THE RESONANCE PRINCIPLE

UNDERSTANDING YOUR LIFE PATH

PHIL HOLMES

authorHOUSE®

AuthorHouse™
1663 Liberty Drive, Suite 200
Bloomington, IN 47403
www.authorhouse.com
Phone: 1-800-839-8640

First published by AuthorHouse 12/18/2007

ISBN: 978-1-4343-5284-2 (sc)

Printed in the United States of America
Bloomington, Indiana

This book is printed on acid-free paper.

THE
RESONANCE
PRINCIPLE

Understanding YOUR Life Path

Phil Holmes

Contents

Dedication:

Dear Emma,

I wish that I knew what I know now, when I was younger.

I hope that the contents of these pages, in some way, help you to understand the life upon which you are embarking.

As my Dad used to tell me, with all advice, you can either accept it, amend it or reject it. I'll leave it to you to decide what you feel is the most appropriate.

Remember, nothing happens by chance. Every person, and all the events in your life are there because you have drawn them there – what you choose to do with them is up to you.

Good luck, and never lose your sense of humour!!

I'll see you again – in another time and in another place.

Love,

Dad

A note from the author

The subject of spirituality and your life path can be complex to understand. Throughout this book I have tried to simplify these complex notions as much as possible, but inevitably, with a topic such as this, it still does require a degree of effort from the reader.

Whilst simplified, the subject matter discussed in chapter 1 is the most complex and I would urge the reader to persevere because the ideas explained in this chapter provide a back drop to the ideas explained in the other chapters.

Some people are already open to this subject-matter, others are still searching to find material which they can relate to. Many people, with whom I have shared the content of these pages, have found it enormously beneficial when trying to understand their own life. I would, therefore, urge you to try to keep an open mind until you have read the whole book.

Phil Holmes
October 2007

Introduction

Why are you here?

What is the purpose of your life?

How do relationships work?

What happens when you die?

I have always been fascinated by questions of "Purpose" and "Universe" and "Life". In recent years the exploration of these questions seems to have taken on a greater urgency for me. Their power is like a strong gravitational force, drawing me towards them, compelling me to investigate further.

In my journey I have tried to understand what spirit is, and how it works. I have tried to understand the difference between spirit and soul, and in this book, I have tried to explain how the process of spirit and the mechanics of the soul interact to create the challenges we each face on a day-to-day basis in our own lives.

My main motivation for writing this book is to provide a guide for my daughter Emma, who at time of writing is 7 years old. My journey towards spirit has taken me many years of exploration, contemplation and investigation, the outcome of which has been distilled into these pages. There is no doubt that the journey itself has been valuable, (although at times I wish it could have been easier), but with hindsight having a guide which would have helped me to understand the broader context of my experiences would have been very useful.

So, having taken years to process so much material, I wanted to produce a guide that is not only easier to understand, but also provides more insight into life circumstances and events so that if Emma feels drawn to investigate her own journey of spirit, then there will be a trail that she can follow and hopefully integrate with the memories of the conversations we will have on this subject.

It is probable that from my current level of consciousness I may never fully understand the journey of spirit, but this book outlines my journey towards spirit. It details the tools and techniques that I have developed, amended or used to facilitate and understand my own journey, such as it is. It represents the sum total of my thinking to date.

I hope you also find it useful for your journey.

Part 1 – The Journey of Spirit

Chapter 1: Spirituality

The journey of spirit is a journey towards consciousness. It is an evolutionary process designed to develop us from the lowest level of consciousness (unconsciousness), to the highest level of consciousness (universal consciousness).

This journey is facilitated by the process of spirituality which uses a hierarchical framework divided into a number of different dimensions each designed to vibrate at increasing frequency rates, thereby facilitating ever-increasing levels of complexity, which facilitate increasingly complex learning experiences.

Let me explain how this process works using the outline of the spiritual hierarchy shown in diagram 1.

THE SPIRITUAL HIERARCHY

7th Heaven	Level 16 Universal Source		13th Dimension
	Level 15 Seraphim	1st order of Angels	12th Dimension
6th Heaven (1st Choir)	Level 14 Cherubim	2nd order of Angels	11th Dimension
	Level 13 Thrones	3rd order of Angels	10th Dimension
	Level 12 Dominions	4th order of Angels	9th Dimension
5th Heaven (2nd Choir)	Level 11 Virtues	5th order of Angels	8th Dimension
	Level 10 Powers	6th order of Angels	7th Dimension
	Level 9 Principalities	7th order of Angels	6th Dimension
4th Heaven (3rd Choir)	Level 8 Archangels	8th order of Angels	5th Dimension
	Level 7 Angels & Guardian Angels	9th order of Angels	4th Dimension
3rd Heaven	Level 6 Human	1st order of Mortality	3rd Dimension
2nd Heaven	Level 5 Animal	2nd order of Mortality	3rd Dimension
	Level 4 Plant	3rd order of Mortality	3rd Dimension
	Level 3 Molecular	1st order of Elements	2nd Dimension
1st Heaven	Level 2 Atomic	2nd order of Elements	1st Dimension
	Level 1 Sub-Atomic	3rd order of Elements	1st Dimension

Diagram 1: The Spiritual Hierarchy

The Spiritual Hierarchy

The lowest level of experience within the hierarchy – level 1 in the 1st dimension - is known as the "**Sub-Atomic**" level, (which is the 3rd order of elements). This level relates to the "fundamental" particles which are the building blocks of the universe.

On this level, fundamental particles such as neutrinos and gluons exist within infinitesimally small spheres of influence and evolve by bonding with and maintaining orbits around more complex particles such as quarks, mesons, baryons, hadrons and leptons. Not until a sub-atomic particle has mastered orbital movement, can it then evolve to the next level.

Level 2 - the "**Atomic**" level (2nd order of elements), the baryons, hadrons and leptons evolve to form photons, protons, neutrons and electrons.

On level 3 – the "**Molecular**" level, (1st order of Elements), is comprised of 105 sub-levels which represent all the chemical elements in the periodic table. On this level, atoms evolve by learning how to cooperate, combine and co-exist in harmony with other atoms in order to create new states of energy – molecules - that have more than one part, for example, when 2 hydrogen atoms and 1 oxygen atom merge to form a water molecule (H_2O). Since the ability to bond with and create consistent chemical reactions with other energy forms is a prerequisite for the next level, it is only once this has been mastered that molecules can progress from level 3 to level 4 (i.e. from the 2nd dimension into the 3rd dimension).

The objective of our journey through the three orders of Elements (1st heaven) is to develop the capability of sustaining a base for cellular structures which are required on the next phase of development.

On level 4 – the "**Plant**" level, (the 3rd order of Mortality), we evolve from the 2nd dimension into the 3rd dimension where "biological" molecules are shaped into forms that appear to live and die, i.e. the appearance of mortality. This level of consciousness contains literally millions of sub-levels relating to each species of plant. The learning on this level evolves from the creating of chemical compounds on the previous level to learning about how we use these chemical compounds to create cell structures, and then learning the more complicated process of "growing" cells by sub-dividing cell structures to create physical growth against a DNA blueprint.

On this level, we begin to learn how to interact with other universal systems – such as through the process of photosynthesis, which links the Sun and the Earth. We learn how to develop roots that can reach down into the earth and convert molecular compounds such as water into cell structures with the DNA profile to form the shape, colour and fragrance of leaves or flowers. This is the first level of sensory perception, such as making sound, as a tree does through the rustling of leaves and through plants such as the "Venus fly trap" reacting to the sense of touch to catch its prey. On this level, we begin to understand the process of basic reproduction through the creation and dispersion of seeds and spores. Because this is the entry level for understanding mortality, we also begin to learn about the cyclical nature of the universe, through experiencing seasons, in which some plants are born, grow, wither and die before being regenerated anew the next season. Since the knowledge to form basic cell structures is a pre-requisite for the next level of evolution, this level requires to be mastered before we can move on.

On level 5 – the **"Animal"** level, (the 2nd order of mortality), we evolve from simple cell organisms to more complex cellular organisms which develop a much greater range of sensory perception. The learning on this level starts with the creation of nerve cells and synapses which, when excited by external events or stimuli, register these perceptions by sending electrical impulses along neurotransmitters to a central processing point, or brain.

On this level there are millions of sub-levels in the forms of insects and animals which are used as vehicles to experience. These vehicles range from the tiniest bug, that will experience limited sensory perception for only a few hours and perhaps within only a few square centimetres, to the largest of animals, like an elephant, that will experience and learn sensory perception over many years and over hundreds of square miles.

As well as learning about movement (for example stalking or migration), the learning on this level will also encompass hearing, sight, sound, smell and limited vocal communication. A key part of this level includes the journey from wild animal to a domestic animal because the proximity to the human kingdom allows domestic animals to view the human environment at close quarters before participating on the next level. It is our capacity to interpret and respond to the electrical synapses between cells, (produced in response to external stimuli), which facilitates increased levels of consciousness and allow us to evolve from the animal level to the more complex environment of the human level.

Level 6 is the "**Human**" level, (the 1st order of mortality).

The human body is made up essentially from: oxygen (65%), carbon (18%), hydrogen (10%), nitrogen (3%), phosphorus (1%), calcium (1.6%), potassium (0.35%), sulphur (0.25%), chlorine (0.15%), sodium (0.15%), magnesium (0.05%), iron (0.008%), iodine (0.00004%), with even smaller traces of copper, zinc, manganese, cobalt, lithium, strontium, aluminium, silicon, lead, arsenic, chromium, tin, fluorine, selenium, vanadium, molybdenum and uranium.

These elements comprise the five billion, billion, billion atoms in the human body, which, in turn, form the 100 trillion cells in the body which, in turn, form the organs, bones and nerves in the body. But other than these chemicals, nothing exists. The human body is nothing but a cocktail of chemicals, which is why in order to form a human body it is necessary to understand at a fundamental level how to balance all of these chemical elements, that is, to have mastered the lessons learned on the previous evolutionary levels.

On this level, the sensory and growth experiences are taken to the next stage and the mind is developed from the fairly primitive state in the animal level into a more elaborate vehicle for consciousness. As well as adding to the range of experiences encountered in the animal realm, there is an increase in the communication experiences through voice and speech. There is also further opportunity to develop our consciousness primarily through the experiencing of emotions such as love, hate, happiness, sadness, rage and jealousy. A more detailed description of the dynamics on the human level is outlined in chapter 2.

Absolute control of the mind and thought processes generated in response to the stimulus of the senses is required in order to progress from the 3rd dimension into the 4th dimension, because in the 4th dimension our thoughts are instantly manifested. This is why mastery of mind and thought processes play such an important role in 3rd dimensional experiences.

The evolution of consciousness so far, therefore, is outlined in diagram 2.

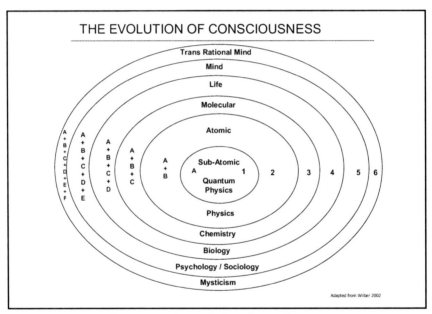

Diagram 2 - The Evolution of Consciousness

The critical point to remember here, is that each layer of consciousness transcends, *but evolves from*, the previous layer, thereby increasing the degree of complexity associated with each layer.

The **Atomic** layer transcends but includes the **Sub-Atomic** layer, i.e. all neutrons and electrons are made up from quarks but not all quarks evolve into electrons or neutrons. Similarly, whilst all **molecules** are made up from **atoms**, not all atoms evolve into molecules. On the life layer, whilst all **Life** evolves from molecules, not all molecules are capable of supporting Life.

The **Mind** layer transcends but evolves from the layer of **Life**. On this layer, life has evolved to a stage that is capable of rational thought. As such, all levels of **Mind** evolve from **Life** but not all **Life** is capable of supporting **Mind**, e.g. fungus or amoebas are alive, but do not have the capacity for rational thought.

The layer of **Trans-Rational Mind** transcends but evolves from the layer of **Mind** and at this level the mind has evolved from a state that is capable of rational thought to a state that can transcend the ego, and can begin to become capable of trans-rational thought.

The disciplines of physics, biology, psychology and sociology attempt to explain the world through the study of the layers of **Matter, Life** and **Mind**, but this approach produces a fragmented view of consciousness. In recent years, quantum physics is beginning to show that everything in the universe – whether it be a wall, a stone, a tree or a human – is simply, at its lowest level, constructed of matter vibrating at a specific rate and, moreover, is also beginning to discover that this matter is affected by what quantum physicists are now calling "non-local consciousness". It is only by attempting to understand the process of spirituality that humanity may move closer to uncovering the highest universal truths.

The next levels in the spiritual hierarchy relate to dimensions that we can have very little direct knowledge of. These levels are often referred to as "the 9 orders of angels"– because these levels form the collective realms of spirit – where time and physical form alter.

The 4th dimension is not a physical realm, and consequently does not require a physical body. The lower levels of this realm can be accessed by transcending the physical realm. Only a few humans – those we label as mystics or gurus or enlightened - can consistently achieve this state through fasting, meditation, prayer or other practices. Others, however, have caught a glimpse of this state of being through either an out-of-body experience or a near death experience.

Level 7 – "**Angels**" (9th order of angels) refers to entities whose primary function is to help and guide elements in the Atomic, Molecular and Plant realms, that comprise of all of the states of being within the 1st and 2nd dimensions. This level also includes "**Guardian Angels**" – where the learning relates to watching over the affairs of mortals by helping and guiding beings currently on the 3rd dimension, primarily humans.

Level 8 – "**Archangel**" (8th order of angels). The experiences on this level relate to acting as a guide for Angels and Guardian Angels.

Level 9 - "**Principalities**" (7th order of angels) are guardians of nations and look after collective elements in the 3rd dimension such as cities, towns or countries and act as guides to facilitate the evolution of the archangels.

Level 10 - "**Powers**" (6th order of angels) are responsible for the laws of karma, birth and death, i.e. the border between heaven and earth. At death it is the Powers who have the responsibility to oversee our transition from the human plane back into the spiritual plane (this process is explained in more detail in the next chapter).

Level 11 - "**Virtues**" (5th order of angels) are responsible for spiritual light, for grace and valour and act as guides for the evolution of the Powers.

Level 12 - "**Dominions**" (4th order of angels) are responsible for the spiritual hierarchy and for mercy and act as guides for the evolution of the Virtues.

Level 13 - "**Thrones**" (3rd order of angels) are responsible for the planets; they create channels or rays of incoming and outgoing energies. They ensure that these energies flow through the realms. They have the responsibility of illuminating injustice throughout the physical realms and dispensing justice with perfect objectivity. They also act as guides to facilitate the evolution of the Dominions.

Level 14 - "**Cherubim**" (2nd order of angels) are the guardians of the stars and the heavens and act as guides to facilitate the evolution of the Thrones.

Level 15 - "**Seraphim**" (1st order of angels) occupy the highest rank in the nine orders of angels, and as such, surround the Universal Source and maintain the vibration of creation by directing the divine energy that emanates from the Source. They are beings of pure light and are charged with keeping divinity in perfect order as well as acting as guides for the Cherubim.

Level 16 – "**Universal Source**" (the Source) - When a being evolves to the level of universal consciousness, the next phase of its development involves learning about omnipotence (being all powerful), omniscience (being all knowing), omnipresence (being everywhere), and supreme benevolence (being all loving). In order to learn about this, however, the Source needs to create a new environment within which this learning can take place.

At the beginning of our universe, therefore, there was only the Source, with an objective to design and create an environment that would allow it to learn about its absolute state of being. In order to do this however, the Source had to create an environment that is "relative" to itself so that it could experience all that it "is" by contrasting this with all that it "is not"

For example, in the relative environment of the 3rd dimension, we can only experience the notion of "hot" by linking it with the notion of "cold", i.e. hot only becomes a valid concept in relation to the concept we know as cold. Similarly, we can only experience "up" through "down" and "left" through "right". So, in order for the Source to experience being all-powerful, (omnipotence), it had to also create the state we call "powerless". Similarly, omnipresence or being everywhere could only be experienced by creating a state known as "somewhere". To experience "all knowing" (omniscience), a state known as "ignorance" had to be created, and to experience "supreme benevolence" a state known as "supreme malevolence", or evil, had to be created. These "opposite" states of being form continuums against which the source experience its own divinity and against which our level of consciousness can be continually assessed. Our universe provides just such a relative environment.

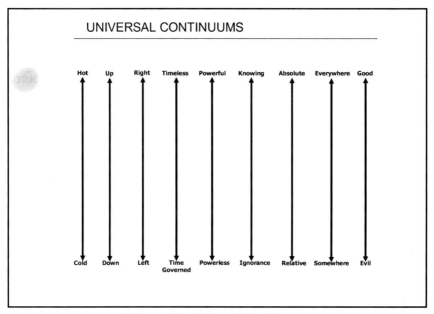

Diagram 3 – Universal Continuums

Having created a relative environment, the Source needed a mechanism through which it could experience all there was to experience. But, because the Source was all that there was, then the Source had to take a portion of its own energy and divide this portion of its own energy into countless fragments of lesser energy, in order to create a countless number of conduits for experiencing. (This process of division is where the notion of "Father" and "Son" comes from in the religious texts).

This process of the Source dividing itself works rather like a hologram. In the same way that, if broken, each fragment of a hologram contains a picture of the whole, the same is true of the process used by the Source when creating fragments of itself. Each fragment of the Source retains a connection to the Source through a "Source Particle". It is this elementary particle that keeps each of the fragments in touch with the Source, and the Source in touch with each of its fragments. Each of these fragments of the Source currently represents itself as part of the many varieties of atoms, molecules, plants, animals and humans that we see around us, as well as all of the other forms that exist in other dimensions. Each fragment - or entity - continuously feeds back data in the form of thoughts, words, actions, emotions and experiences in order that the Source can learn a bit more about each fragment of its being.

Once the design for this relative environment was complete, the Source needed to put the plan into action – to start the ball rolling. In order to begin, therefore, the Source had to "separate" a portion of its own energy to create a universal body suitable for experiential learning. The Source chose to do this through a one-off event – a singularity – and it was this process of creating the universal body that science now commonly refers to as "The Big Bang".

When faced with the prospect of designing a universe with all the energy systems and life forms contained within it, the bandwidth of potential experiences across this universe is vast. So vast, in fact, that it is necessary to divide the bandwidth of universal experience into sub-sections, or dimensions, within which appropriate parameters for experiencing could be applied. This structure is the spiritual hierarchy shown in diagram 1.

The universe, therefore, is a feedback mechanism within which each entity uses its "Source particle" as a conduit to feed back sensory data to the Source, in order that it, in turn, can better understand itself and thus, learn about omniscience, omnipotence, omnipresence and supreme benevolence.

The Source needed some rules to ensure that the experiences could be controlled in a consistent way, so it created the universal laws. These laws are what our scientists have spent the last 1,000 years discovering. The laws of physics, cosmology, chemistry, biology, psychology and the laws of spirituality. From a spiritual perspective, one of the most significant of the universal laws is the Law of Karma. It is the principle of cause and effect or "you reap as you sow", because this underpins all experiences in this universe. The Law of Karma is explained in more detail in chapter 10.

Once the separation had begun, it would take hundreds of millions of years of interaction (in Earth time) before our universe would evolve into its current state. During this time, however, whilst the rules may have stayed consistent, the environment and the feedback mechanisms have evolved considerably, and it is the interaction of these three elements - the environment, the rules and the entities - that create the process we know as "Life".

At present, each fragment of the Source – each entity - is at a different level in its own evolutionary journey – and that includes each of us – because we form part of this universal mosaic. And this is why our desire to return to the Source is fundamental in all of us, and why sooner or later, we feel compelled to begin searching – to understand our journey of spirit.

This spiritual process continues until the energy level or the "vibrational" level of each fragment of the Source is the same as that of the Source itself, at that point, the fragment can then merge once again with the Source, thereby returning "home" – having experienced all there was to experience. Each time a fragment of the Source returns "home", the Source then knows a little bit more of itself. When all portions of the Source have returned "home", then the Source will have experienced all that there is to experience, with every fragment of its being.

This is the journey of spirit. This re-merging with the Source is the culmination of the spiritual journey. This re-merging is what each of us has longed for across aeons.

The Oxford English Dictionary defines "spirit" in the following way:

SPIRIT /'spirit/n & v – n
1. *The vital animating essence of a person or animal. The intelligent non-physical part of a person; the soul;*
2. *A rational or intelligent being without a body. Supernatural being such as a ghost, fairy, etc;*
3. *A person's mental or moral nature or qualities.*

I define spirit (and consequently spirituality) in a slightly different way, however:

SPIRIT

1. *The Source and origin of universal consciousness;*
2. *A frequency range for energy;*
3. *The collective description for Souls.*

SPIRITUALITY

1. *The process for the evolution of consciousness.*

Chapter 2: The Journey of Soul

The concepts of spirit and soul are often used interchangeably, as if they represent the same thing, and this caused confusion in my mind when I first began to explore the topic of spirituality. So, having outlined what I believe spirit is, I believe that it is now necessary to explain how the notion of spirit relates to the notion of soul.

Soul: A Definition

The Oxford English dictionary defines soul in the following way:

SOUL/n

1. *An individual; not a soul, life and soul, poor soul, etc;*
2. *The personification or pattern of something (soul of discretion);*
3. *The spiritual or immaterial part of a human being, often regarded as immortal.*

I would define soul in a different way, however:

SOUL

1. *A fragment of the Source;*
2. *An evolving portion of energy relating to an individual entity (person, animal, plant, etc) over which they have stewardship;*
3. *A conduit for spirit.*

As explained in the previous chapter, when the universe was created, the Source took a portion of its own energy and divided it into many fragments, which collectively represent all the matter there is in the universe. Each fragment acts as a conduit for the Source to experience itself in all its forms. Each fragment is designed specifically to act as a mechanism to feed back learning and experiences to the Source. Each fragment has been specifically designed to contribute to the **Source's On-going Understanding of Life**, hence the term **SOUL**.

The evolution of each soul, (each fragment of the Source), takes place over many aeons, but the overarching purpose for any soul is to merge once more with the Source. This merging with the Source can only be achieved, however, once the energy profile and vibrational rate of the soul is the same as that of the Source. Until the vibrational patterns are the same, a soul cannot be re-united with the Source – it cannot complete its journey. And the only way for the soul to raise its vibrational profile is through experiential learning. The journey of the soul, therefore, requires each soul to continually grow its own vibrational rate until it is at an appropriate level, and can merge once more with the Source.

Each soul begins its journey at the lowest level of consciousness on the spiritual hierarchy, and evolves to overcome challenges and lessons - firstly in the sub-atomic realm, then the atomic realm, then the molecular realm, the plant realm, the animal realm, the human realm, and ultimately through the higher levels of the realm of spirit, until each soul has grown sufficiently and is capable of rejoining the Source, and thereby returning home.

There is a degree of hubris in our society that perceives humans as being the most evolved species in the universe. A common perspective is that humans are, in some way, special. When looked at from the perspective of the spiritual hierarchy however, we come to realise that, rather than humans being the pinnacle of evolution we are, in fact, quite low down on the evolutionary ladder, with a long way to go in terms of spiritual development.

Once a soul attains the level on the spiritual hierarchy that relates to human consciousness, it utilises a "personality" or an "ego" as a key part of the learning associated with this level of development. The "Circle of Life" framework which is explained in the next chapter was developed in order to simplify this process.

Chapter 3: The Circle of Life

The lyrics of the song "The Circle of Life", written by Tim Rice for the soundtrack to the Disney film "The Lion King", are a good way to begin to understand this process:

> **"From the day we arrive on the planet,**
> **and blinking step into the sun,**
> **there's more to see than can ever be seen,**
> **more to do than can ever be done.**
> **There's far too much to take in here.**
> **More to find than can ever be found.**
> **But the sun rolling high through the sapphire sky,**
> **keeps the great and the small on an endless round.**
> **It's the circle of life, and it moves us all.**
> **Through despair and hope.**
> **Through faith and love.**
> **'till we find our place, on a path unwinding.**
> **It's the circle..... the circle of life....."**

Remember, the overarching objective as we journey across the aeons is to increase the vibrational rate of our soul (our fragment of the Source), to a point where it can merge back with the Source. Given that this can only be achieved through encountering and transcending experiences in each of the dimensions (as outlined in the spiritual hierarchy), then it is necessary to expose the fragment of the Source over which we have stewardship, our soul, to a wide range of experiences, both positive and negative.

Because this universe offers too much to experience in one lifetime, however, it is necessary to "chunk" this task down into a range of smaller experiences, and repeat the process again and again, and again, until we have managed to raise the vibrational rate of our soul to a level that allows our soul to evolve from one dimension to the next (in our case, from the 3rd dimension into the 4th dimension), and then continue to repeat the process until we eventually reach the same level as the Source.

On the human level of the spiritual hierarchy, this process of cosmic recycling is known as "reincarnation". If the idea of reincarnation feels uncomfortable to you, I would ask you to keep your mind open as you read this chapter. The philosophy of reincarnation forms part of the belief systems of around 70% of the world's population, and was even part of Christian doctrine until around 325 A.D., at which point it was removed by the decree of the first ecumenical council held at Nicea, and replaced by the Nicean creed used in Christian services to this day.

At the beginning of the universe each soul began with a clean slate. Ahead lay a vast number of potential experiences across many dimensions. The life we are currently experiencing is simply our latest attempt to achieve a level of mastery over 3rd dimensional experiences, and in so doing, to be able to evolve as a spiritual being. I have simplified this process, as it applies to 3rd dimensional experiences, into 9 key stages that are outlined in diagram 4 and explained in more detail in chapters 4 through 12.

THE CIRCLE OF LIFE

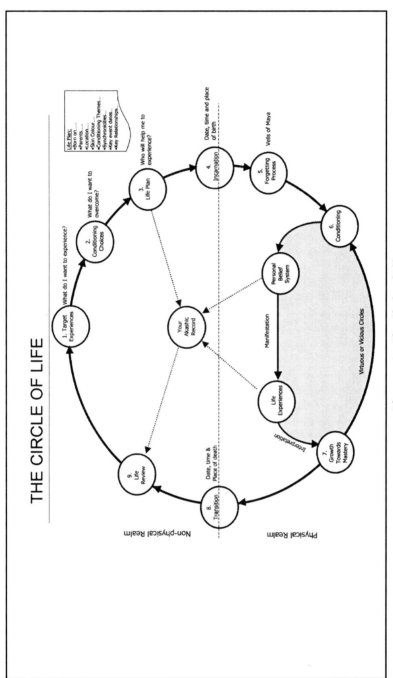

Diagram 4 – The Circle of Life

Chapter 4: Target Experiences

Whilst in the realm of spirit, our energy is "anchored" to a vibrational frequency that reflects our stage of spiritual development. In the realm of spirit, there is no pressure to progress with our development, there is nothing that we "need" to do. There is, however, an inherent desire within our being to return to the Source, and it is this longing that drives each of us to pursue learning through experience.

Within the realm of spirit is the only place where true "free will" actually operates. Only from this place can we choose exactly what we want to experience, and where we want to experience it. When a soul is deciding what it wishes to experience next, it can choose from any experience or range of experiences, in any universe that relates to its current stage of evolution. Or, the soul can decide to choose not to experience anything: this is true free will.

The option for a soul to choose from any experience in any universe is possible because, at its most basic level, universal consciousness exists as a possibility field. Each choice made by a soul, therefore, narrows down this possibility field.

Once a soul chooses what it wants to experience, where it wants to experience it, and over which timeframe it wishes to experience it, then the "bandwidth" of free will narrows in line with these choices and this is reflected in the narrowing of the bandwidth of the possibility field.

An example of this is outlined in diagram 5.

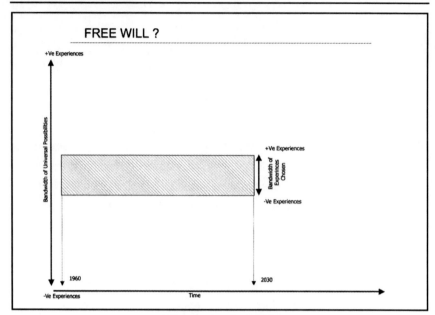

FREE WILL ?

Diagram 5 – Free Will

In the realm of spirit, (as outlined in the spiritual hierarchy), there are many entities that act as guides and helpers to those on lower levels of vibration. The role of these guides is to help each soul decide what lessons it needs to learn in order to best achieve the level of soul growth desired. The more a soul wants to get out of an incarnation, then the more extreme the set of experiences will be. Alternatively, the easier a soul wants an incarnation to be, the easier the lessons and experiences will be, but the lower the level of growth.

As an example, let's say that after discussions with its guide, a soul decides that in order to grow further, it needs to increase its understanding of a number of specific states of being. It may decide that it needs to increase its experience of the state of being labelled "**humility**", as well as the state labelled "**persistence**" and the state of being labelled "**courage**". So, having decided on these primary experiences for this lifetime the soul now has a broad theme for the life upon which it will shortly embark – let's call this theme "**triumph over adversity**".

Having chosen a set of target experiences, the soul then progresses to the next stage in the Circle of Life – Conditioning Choices.

22

Chapter 5: Conditioning Choices

Having decided on the overarching theme (triumph over adversity), and the primary themes (in this example the three themes of humility, persistence and courage), the next stage is to define how the soul will be conditioned in the early part of its life, i.e. does it want to make this incarnation easy or difficult? (Remember, the easier it is, the lower the level of growth, and the harder it is, the greater the level of growth). The choices made during this phase will determine how the belief system is constructed, because it is our belief system that will facilitate the consistent attraction of events and experiences, through which the soul can attempt to "learn" how to transcend these experiences.

The belief system will largely be created as a result of the soul's childhood development exposure – its conditioning profile – so it is necessary to choose the method and extent of the conditioning, as well as to choose which characters in the forthcoming life will set up this conditioning profile.

Within this phase, therefore, a soul will work with its guide to determine the "depth" for its life themes. For example: if a soul had previously struggled with being humble, and perhaps had lived the last few incarnations as an arrogant person (which is why it has chosen to try again with this experience), the soul may choose an easier path by being conditioned by extremely humble parents, in humble circumstances, in order to have the best possible chance of understanding humility from an early age. Or, conversely, the soul could choose to be conditioned by extremely arrogant parents, in order that the conditioning profile makes it more difficult for the soul to understand and deal with issues of humility.

Once the soul has finalised the manner in which it will be conditioned, it is time to move on to the next phase – designing a Life Plan.

Chapter 6: Your Life Plan

The construction of a detailed life plan relies upon the help of others. As we journey across the aeons we do not do so alone, we journey in groups. Within the realm of spirit there are many levels of vibration within each dimension. In order to assist us in our growth, entities at the same vibrational level are banded together in groups ranging in size from twelve to twenty. These groups are known as "soul groups". Our soul group is the group of souls with whom we act out many of our incarnational experiences (like our spiritual family).

In the process of designing a life path, a soul works very closely with its guide or guides, and makes extensive use of what is known as the "Planning Room". The Planning Room can best be thought of as a cosmic rehearsal room, in which a soul can "try on" different personality types, as well as different physical profiles, to see which profiles might best suit the aspirations it has for its forthcoming life.

At this stage in designing a life plan a soul can either choose from countless numbers of predefined personalities, or it can choose to create a new personality. When a soul decides to choose a predefined personality, it is rather like an actor choosing to play the role of a particular character in the theatre. If we consider all the plays that have ever been written, there are thousands of characters an actor could choose from. Choosing characters for a life plan is a similar process, but on a cosmic scale.

Because time does not exist in the realm of spirit, all the predefined personalities are available to be played over and over again, by any soul that wishes to experience the attributes a pre-defined personality has to offer. This is why there are many cases documented by therapists who perform past life regressions on different clients having experienced "being" the same personality in a past life. This is the equivalent of many different actors saying they have played Hamlet or some other well known character. Because the personality of characters have been pre-defined, any and every soul can choose to experience the personality traits of this character, if it fits with the way they wish to grow at any given time. This means that all the personalities ever created are available for any soul to reuse if they so choose.

If a soul wishes to create a new personality, then it is also free to do so, and it starts by determining the **genetic** profile - because this will determine its physical characteristics - and then the **memetic** profile - because this will determine its behavioural characteristics. When selecting a genetic profile, a soul can choose from the predetermined genetic pool, a process that science is currently unravelling. In doing so, the soul chooses: physical attributes and defects, skin colour, health and sickness characteristics, blood type, metabolic characteristics, and so on. When selecting the memetic profile, the soul chooses from a predetermined range of characteristics that will then determine the motivations and behaviours of the character, once integrated with the genetic profile choices.

In choosing the memetic profile, there are four critical elements that influence behavioural patterns during an incarnation. These are: the date of birth, the time of birth, the place of birth, and the birth name. These four elements are chosen specifically because it is through these choices that universal energies are aligned in a unique way that impacts upon the physical, mental, intellectual and emotional states of the personality. Let me explain how this works.

Date and Time of Birth
Each of the chemical elements that make up the human body is linked with, and directly affected by, a broader universal body. For example, the movement of the moon through the heavens affects water, and the effects of these moon cycles on tidal movements are well documented. Given that the human body is comprised of approximately 70% water (which in turn is made from the elements hydrogen and oxygen), then it should come as no surprise to find out that the cycles of the moon also have an impact upon human behaviour – and again, the effects of moon cycles on human

26

behaviour are well documented elsewhere.

In the same way as the position of the moon in its heavenly orbit affects how the elements of hydrogen and oxygen behave, so too do the movements of each of the other planets separately impact upon the other chemical elements that make up the human body. Research is now beginning to suggest that the movements of Saturn impact upon the element of lead, which in turn is linked to the emotion of anger; and in a similar way, the element of mercury links to the emotion of irritation, aluminium links to sorrow and zinc to stress.

As the planets continue to move through space, their gravitational pull becomes weaker or stronger and this exerts either weaker or stronger forces upon the elements within the human body, which in turn affects how we, as humans, feel and behave. As the dance of the planets evolves on a minute-by-minute, hour-by-hour, day-by-day basis, the pattern of influence is therefore reflected in our human chemical structure, which in turn influences how we feel, think and behave. It is the dance of the planets, therefore, that determines our individual harmonic and biorhythmic profiles on a moment-to-moment basis.

This cosmic imprint, i.e. the specific location of the planets in orbit at the exact time of our birth, acts as an anchor point for the cosmic energy pattern of the soul, and uses the specific date and time of birth to create a unique starting point from which our human harmonics and biorhythms can begin (harmonics is explained further in chapter 16). The date of birth is also specifically selected because it is through this choice that details of the life path of the soul can be encoded (see chapter 13 for more details).

Place of Birth
The choice of birth place is important from a spiritual perspective because each country, and even each region within each country, was created to facilitate different types of experience.

On the Earth, each country vibrates at a slightly different rate, and each region vibrates at a tone relative to that set by the country, either slightly higher or slightly lower, and each town or city at a rate relative to the region. It is the interaction of the vibrational frequencies of the country, the region, the town and the individual soul that facilitates particular sets of experience.

In the developed world, typical life plan themes include: family, job, finances, health, diet, education, friends, attitude, material possessions and spirituality. In less developed countries, however, the portfolio of experience is likely to relate to more basic experiences, but also more intense themes, such as survival, food or health.

For example, Scotland as a country has a fairly low level of vibration which leads, in general, to negativity within the culture, and contributes to the country's "sick man of Europe" image. Regions, cities, towns, districts and neighbourhoods then all vibrate at a tone either slightly higher or slightly lower than the tone set by the country. If the vibrational tone of a region is slightly higher than that of the country, this leads to a general perception of the place being a "good" place to live, and where the vibrational tone is lower than that of the country, this leads to a general perception of the place being a "bad" place to live.

When a soul is choosing a location within which to be born, a key consideration therefore, is the vibrational tone of the country and region, since these will enhance the intensity of the life experience. This is why, when a soul in the form of a personality emigrates from one country to another, it often finds much higher degrees of success. This is because the vibrational profile of the region and country the personality was born into is likely to have been in conflict with the personality's vibrational profile, which then leads to an energy conflict between the personality and the region, resulting in negative outcomes. Assuming that the personality immigrates to a town in a region and in a country which has a more harmonious tone, a lot of the energy conflict can be avoided, and greater success achieved. History is littered with thousands of cases in which people who, having achieved no success in the country of their birth, went on to achieve overwhelming success in all areas of their lives, once they relocated to a new environment.

Birth Name

In the same way that each country resonates at a different frequency, so too does each forename, middle name and surname given to the personality after their birth. The name by which a soul will be known during its incarnation is selected in the planning phase, because the birth name chosen sets up a unique vibrational profile that encodes the key themes of the life plan (these concepts are explained further in chapter 14).

The Detailed Plan

So, having decided on the date, time and place of birth, as well as our birth name, the next stage is to decide upon the other key elements that are required in order to provide the details and colour to our life plan.

It is necessary to decide who, from our current soul group, will play the roles of mother and father or guardians. These characters, in turn, will not only adopt the genetic profile chosen by the soul (to ensure the appropriate DNA structure as a human, and therefore determine the physical attributes and weaknesses the soul wishes to experience), but also the memetic profile chosen by the soul (to ensure the soul is exposed to the appropriate conditioning and behavioural patterns).

Once the key roles of parents have been agreed, a soul also chooses who will play the other key roles, such as siblings (if appropriate), partners, colleagues, friends and enemies. The line from Shakespeare's *"As You Like It"* is appropriate to describe the "casting" phase of a life plan.

"All the world is a stage, and in his time, each man plays many parts...."

Once the "cast" has been agreed upon, the next key step in designing a life plan is to decide where in the life plan to place "Probability Anchors", "Resonance Energy" and "Synchronistic Events".

Probability Anchors

Once a soul has narrowed its bandwidth of potential experiences through its initial choices, it must now begin to "lock in" the specifics of the life it will experience for each theme. Within the narrowed bandwidth chosen by the soul, a range of possibilities exist on a continuum ranging from positive experiences through to negative experiences. If, when choosing the specific experiences for this lifetime, a soul chose only negative experiences, this would make for a very difficult lifetime. Similarly, if a soul chose only positive experiences, this would make for a very easy lifetime. In order to harmonise the sets of experiences, therefore, a balance is generally created between positive and negative experiences over a timeline that will be the soul's lifetime on Earth.

We can now return to our example, in which the target experiences chosen relate to learning about "triumph over adversity". The soul needs to choose some adverse circumstances, in order that it can experience them, learn about them and, hopefully, overcome them. In attempting to overcome these circumstances, the soul will be presented with a number of opportunities to experience humility, persistence and courage – which are the lessons considered necessary by the soul for its own growth.

Let me simplify an example to show how this process works.

In order for a soul to experience humility, persistence and courage, it needs to select the themes through which these experiences can be delivered. There are thousands of possible themes, such as: family, relationships, love, hate, envy, greed, power, career, finances and so on. Let's say in our example that the themes chosen by the soul to experience humility, persistence and courage are **love**, **finances**, **career** and **recognition**. Each theme will then be taken one at a time and the soul, with the help of its guide, will create a "profile" for how each theme will present both positive and negative experiences over the lifetime.

When designing the profile for each theme, the soul begins by deciding upon the certain events in the life plan. These points in the life plan are known as "Probability Anchors". A Probability Anchor, therefore, is an event (either positive or negative) relating to a particular life theme that is certain to occur at a specific time during the lifetime of the soul.

Diagram 6 highlights how this could look for the theme of **Love**.

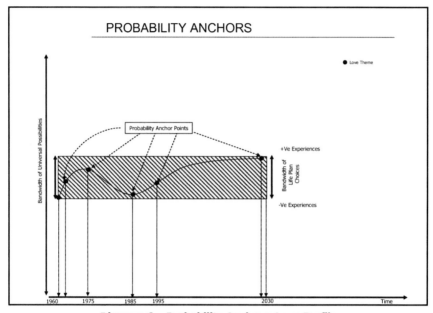

Diagram 6 – Probability Anchors: Love Profile

We can establish from the above profile that when this soul incarnates in 1960 it will have increasingly positive experiences in relation to love in its early years and this will grow until teenage years. At that point the soul will have chosen to begin to have increasingly negative experiences relating to love – perhaps its parents divorce - until the soul experiences an event which is at the very bottom of the bandwidth frequency within which it is operating – perhaps the loss of parent in 1985 - before perhaps meeting a partner in 1995 and then beginning to have more positive experiences, that eventually peak towards the end of this soul's life.

Once the profile for the theme of **Love** has been completed, the process is repeated again for the themes of **Finances, Career,** and **Recognition**.

When these life themes are woven together, the outcome is shown in diagram 7.

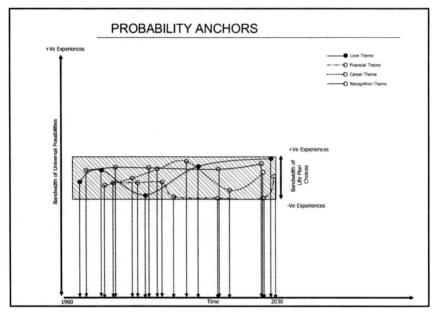

Diagram 7 – Probability Anchors: Full Profile

We can see from the above diagram that, in this example lifetime, all the probability anchors have been fairly evenly spaced, ensuring a fairly even distribution of positive and negative experiences throughout the lifetime.

If, however, a soul wanted a period of either intensely positive or negative experiences, it could cluster several probability anchor points within a condensed timeframe. An example of negative clustering is outlined in diagram 8, where on the love theme the soul loses four members of its Earth family in very short succession, closely followed by a birth and then yet another death, before then increasing steadily throughout the rest of its lifetime.

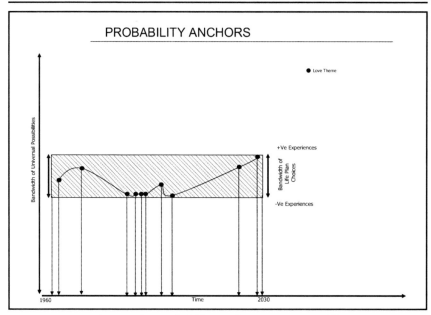

Diagram 8 – Probability Anchors: Intense Profile

On occasions during an incarnation, humans can feel severely challenged because a lot of negative events happen within a short period of time in our life. From a spiritual perspective, however, the clustering of experiences is one way of adding to the intensity of the experience.

A key part of this design phase is to try to create a plan that will ensure spiritual growth, but also ensure that the soul is not overwhelmed by the intensity of the experiences in the physical realm, that could result in sickness, a nervous breakdown or, in extreme cases, even precipitate the soul terminating the incarnation early through suicide.

Manifestation

In a life plan, only the path between any two probability anchor points is flexible, and therefore subject to the laws of manifestation.

If we imagine a life path theme as a piece of string tied loosely between two nails, this forms a close approximation of how a life path is connected between two probability anchor points. Because of the tension in the string, there is a maximum point to which the string can be distorted or pulled – the "stretch point" - and this restricts the degree to which a life path can be altered through the use of manifestation techniques (see diagram 9).

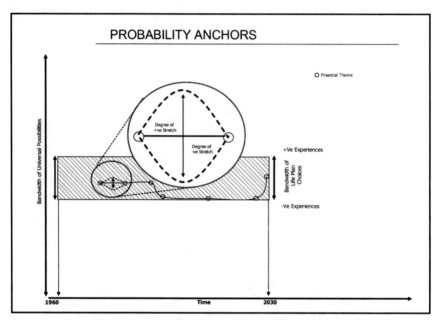

Diagram 9 – Probability Anchors & Manifestation

The reason why manifestation techniques seldom work consistently is because a soul can only manifest experiences that are:

1) Within its chosen bandwidth of experience in this lifetime, and

2) Within the "stretch points" between any two probability anchors.

So this means that if a soul has chosen to experience "poverty" in this lifetime, then it will never experience wealth no matter how much it persists with manifestation techniques, such as goal setting or visualisation exercises. This is explained in more detail in chapter 10.

In addition to the above criteria, manifestation relies upon the other key variables of positive and negative thoughts – which is why our conditioning profile plays a critical role in our life.

From a universal perspective, all outcomes, events or objects require the exact same level of thought in order to manifest – there is no order of magnitude in miracles! In our relative plane, however, every physical manifestation – whether it be an outcome, an event or a physical object – has a "required value" (RV in the equation below), and this required value is directly proportional to the **perceived** value of the outcome, event or object as determined by the conditioning profile of the personality. So, the harder an individual thinks a specific outcome is to manifest, the higher its "required value" will be for the personality, and consequently, the more difficult it will be to achieve. Someone else, however, may consider the same outcome easier to manifest, and consequently for them, its RV will be lower. It is all relative to our conditioning.

The manifestation process brings outcomes into being through the mechanism of thought, either positive or negative thought. You are what you are, you have what you have and you do what you do because you think it! Positive thoughts are typically (although not exclusively) characterised by phrases such as: "I can", "I will", "It can happen" and so on. Conversely, negative thoughts are typically characterised by phrases such as: "I can't", "I won't be able to", "It will never happen to me".

Each time we think about a desired outcome, event or object, we think of it in either a positive or negative way – and sometimes we can alternate between the two perspectives several times within a few seconds before settling on either a positive or a negative thought. Each time we do so, the energy associated with the thought is sent out into the universe – which remember is a probability field - and is added to either our "Total Positive Thought" count (TPT), or our "Total Negative Thought" count (TNT), where these two elements are combined. Positive thoughts move us closer towards manifestation, whilst negative thoughts move us further away.

I formulated a manifestation equation to help me understand this process. The equation reads as follows:

$$\text{Manifestation} = \frac{(TPT - TNT)}{RV}$$

As mentioned previously, because the universe exists as a probability field, outcomes are manifested through the process of thought. The way probability is measured, however, is on a scale from 0 to 1, where 0 equates to no probability – it will never happen - and 1 equates to a certainty – it is guaranteed to happen.

Because manifestation is based upon the laws of probability, therefore, it is only when the net effect of our "Total Positive Thought" count minus our "Total Negative Thought" count reaches the same value as the "Required Value", that the numerator (top number in the equation above) equals the denominator (bottom number) so that the resulting probability equals 1, i.e. a certainty. When this happens, the universal probability field collapses, and the outcome, event or object will manifest in our physical universe.

The time taken to achieve manifestation is as long as it takes for the positive thought processes to overcome the negative thought processes to the extent that it reaches the required value; only then can physical manifestation can be achieved.

Frequently our preferred timeframe for manifestation is different from the Universe's timeframe, but the Universe is never late, and the more we understand this, the more we decrease our sense of frustration with the manifestation process.

Let me use a simple example of finding a parking space in a city centre to explain how this process works.

When we set out into the city for a day's shopping, we may be initially apprehensive about finding a parking space, (perhaps because as part of our conditioning profile our parents used to hate driving in the city and could never find anywhere to park).

The example in table 1 below outlines how the state of probability fluctuates until the ratio between positive thoughts and negative thoughts equals that of the required value, at which point the probability becomes 1 - a certainty. (In this example, we will assume that the required value – RV – for a parking space is 3).

Thought	Formula Impact $M = \dfrac{(TRT - TNT)}{RV}$	Probability	Outcome
1. I will never be able to find a parking meter in the city centre.	$M = \dfrac{(0 - 1)}{3}$	-0.33	No space available
2. I could try the central plaza; there are sometimes parking meters available there.	$M = \dfrac{(1 - 1)}{3}$	0	No space available
3. The city centre is looking quieter than I was expecting. I should be able to park OK.	$M = \dfrac{(2 - 1)}{3}$	0.33	No space available
4. There is a space! I hope the car in front doesn't nip in (which it does).	$M = \dfrac{(2 - 2)}{3}$	0	No space available
5. There are a few more people leaving. I'm sure I can find a space.	$M = \dfrac{(3 - 2)}{3}$	0.33	No space available
6. This looks more promising. I'm sure I will find a space now if I drive around a few times.	$M = \dfrac{(4 - 2)}{3}$	0.66	No space available
7. I am sure I will find a space within the next few minutes.	$M = \dfrac{(5 - 2)}{3}$	1	Space manifests

Table 1: Example of manifestation

The above example is only given to outline how the process works. But even from this simple example, it is easy to see why so many people have difficulty manifesting positive outcomes in their life. So, whilst in the physical realm, if we want to manifest a specific outcome, event or object, it is critical to ensure that our positive thoughts outweigh our negative thoughts. The more we can do this, the sooner we will be able to manifest, (assuming the outcome is achievable through our chosen path in the first place).

For every outcome we manage to successfully manifest, there are likely to be hundreds that we don't. Only when our predefined outcomes coincide with our life path choices can we achieve a desired outcome. Humans tend to have selective memory, however, and we tend to remember only the times when we managed to manifest a specific outcome.

No one can manifest everything they want. As we say in Scotland, "what's for you will not go past you!" If it's on your path, it'll come to you, and if it's not, then it won't – but you're free to make plans. If it's not on your path there's no point getting all worked up about it. The only influence you have is how you influence the degree of "stretch" between the probability anchor points.

Like all universal themes, manifestation operates on a continuum, which starts with "**requirements**" and as we evolve spiritually, these requirements are replaced by "**preferences**", and if our evolution continues, eventually our preferences are replaced by "**acceptance**" as we step aside and allow the flow of life to guide us.

Having chosen the key life themes, and underpinned each theme with probability anchor points, it is now time to inject the plan with resonance energy.

Resonance Energy
The optimum path between any two points is a straight line, which in a spiritual context equates to the path of listening to, and following our heart. However, because our society is currently not structured in a way that facilitates, let alone encourages, this type of behaviour, it is likely that our path between any two probability anchor points will not be a straight line.

In order to overcome these societal pressures, and minimise the fluctuation of the path between probability anchor points, the path can be underpinned by resonance energy. The principle of resonance is, I believe, the key to understanding our purpose and our life path during our time here on Earth. The resonance principle is a universal principle designed to help a soul navigate through the lower dimensions of the universe, where energy profiles are denser. Resonance energy can be thought of as a packet of high-voltage energy, that can vary in size, and which is used to underpin decision points along a life path, in order to maximise the probability of one path being taken in preference to another.

Resonance energy comes in both positive and negative forms. Positive resonance is designed to interact with the underlying energy profile of a soul in order to draw the soul towards it, whilst negative resonance is designed to interact with the underlying profile of a soul in order to push it away. A combination of both of these energy types is used in an attempt to combat both the dense energy of the 3rd dimension and the effects of social conditioning, to keep the soul on a true path.

Let's say, for example, that as the soul designs its life plan, one of the options (paths) it has arranged with another soul from its soul group, who will play the character of its husband, is that they will meet on a particular date, in a place called "Johnny's Bar". Given the distractions and the dense gravitational forces here on Earth, however, it is possible that, once on Earth, such an event could be "forgotten". To maximise the probability of this meeting taking place, therefore, the soul can underpin the specific event in its life plan with positive resonance energy. In order to increase the probability that the soul will turn up at Johnny's bar on that date and meet its future husband, the soul could attach positive resonance energy to the specific date and time as well as the phrase "Johnny's Bar".

The tricky part of an incarnation here on Earth is that, because we have been conditioned to behave in certain ways, even though we invariably recognise when an event or a path resonates with us, we very often ignore this feeling and give preference to our conditioned response. In doing so, we can find ourselves on paths that do not resonate with us, and that make us unhappy.

So, in our example, let's say that on the specified day, when a friend calls to invite us out for a drink to "a new place called Johnny's Bar", we should feel – for some inexplicable reason - "drawn" towards that path, and decide to go to Johnny's Bar that evening.

Because we do not always listen to our heart, our intuition, or whatever resonates with us, it is generally necessary for the soul to develop a "plan B", (and even a Plan C, D, E, and F), which means that if, on this occasion, despite a strong degree of positive resonance persuading us to go to Johnny's Bar, we decide to stay at home, a critical decision point on our life path will have been passed, and the element of the plan relating to "love" or "relationships" now needs to switch to plan B. This means that the person destined to play the role of our husband in this incarnation will not now meet us at Johnny's Bar that night, as per plan A, but rather at Harry's Bar a month later, at which time the phrase would be "Harry's Bar" and this would be re-enforced with an increased amount of resonance energy.

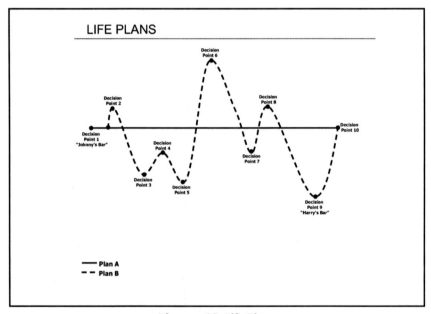

Diagram 10: Life Plans

So, when specific phrases, events, places or names are underpinned with resonance energy and used as part of our life path, they will resonate very strongly with us. In most cases we will not be entirely sure why we feel the need to do a particular thing, or be in a particular place, but this will be because, in our planning phase, we will have designed our plan to give our self the best chance of influencing our decision, in one way or another, through the application of either positive or negative resonance energy.

Synchronistic Events

An additional tool that can be built into a life plan in order to maximise the chances of a soul sticking to an optimal path is the "synchronistic event". Synchronicity can be thought of as a particular set of circumstances which occur as a result of something beyond pure chance – and indeed, that is what it is. Synchronistic events are often used in creating a life plan when a particular decision needs to be made or a particular direction has to be taken. By their very nature, synchronistic events leave the person thinking: "What are the chances of that happening?" and thereby influence decisions.

Synchronistic events are a common form of energy used by the soul to assist the personality during an incarnation. Almost everyone can recall some synchronistic event in their life, such as: meeting an ex-colleague when you are looking for a new job and she is looking to hire someone with exactly your skills and experience.

In essence, your life plan phase is rather like creating your own computer game. You decide who your character is, what he or she will look like and how he or she will be conditioned to behave. You decide where and when the game takes place. You decide which other characters you want to have in your game. You also decide the settings, the parameters and the controls. Overall, however, whilst there are many, many ways in which you can play the game you have designed, you need to realise that ALL possible outcomes for this lifetime have already been considered and built into your life plan!

I believe that the more we can understand about our life plan, the greater our chance of being able to stick to our optimum path. So, relax and enjoy the ride – because the next phase in the Circle of Life is the incarnation phase.

Chapter 7: Incarnation

Once a soul has created a fully detailed plan, the next stage is to move from the spiritual realm into the physical realm in order to execute its plan. In order to do this, there has to be a "step down" in the vibrational rate of the soul's energy pattern. The soul needs to slow down its vibrational rate, in order to anchor itself in a physical body in a 3rd dimensional plane.

The Step-Down Process

This "step-down" process happens in a number of phases. The result of each step-down phase is that a unique layer or imprint is created, each becoming more and more dense, until the physical body is created. Each layer in turn further condenses the energy of the entity until we are left with our dense physical body. Each layer of the body evolves from the previous layer and holds open the channel between the physical and spiritual realms. I have found it most useful to consider the step down process as creating six layers to the body as outlined in diagrams 11 and 12.

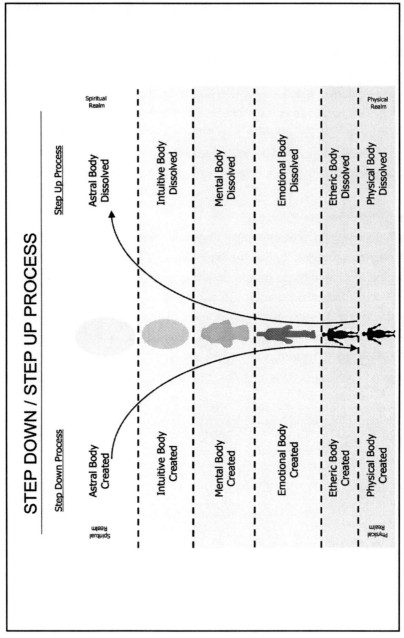

Diagram 11: The Step-Down Process

With each layer – as the human form becomes more defined - there is a further concentration of energy which increases the density and increases the gravitational pull.

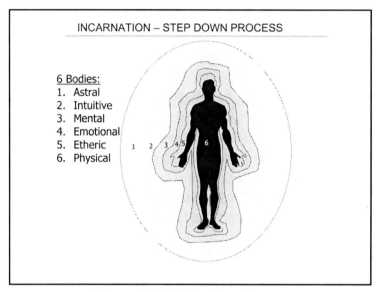

INCARNATION – STEP DOWN PROCESS

6 Bodies:
1. Astral
2. Intuitive
3. Mental
4. Emotional
5. Etheric
6. Physical

Diagram 12: The Step-Down Process

The first phase of step-down creates the **Astral** body that provides the first degree of separation between the realm of spirit and the 3rd dimension.

The second phase of step-down creates the **Intuitive** body that is, in effect, what is known as the "higher self". The intuitive body generates ideas, abstract thoughts and compassion.

The third phase of step-down creates the **Mental** body, which is responsible for processing our conditioning and logic. The fourth phase of step-down creates the **Emotional** body that processes our needs. The fifth phase of step-down creates the **Etheric** body which is very close to the physical body, and processes our nervous system. The sixth phase of step-down creates the **Physical** body that is subsequently used as the vehicle through which sensory perception can be processed and through which an incarnation can be experienced.

As each layer of the body is created, it leaves a slight residue – an aura – which can later be viewed by mystics and healers and allows them to gain more insightful perspectives on the human condition – particularly relating to health issues, since these manifest firstly in the outer bodies and show up as discolouration or distortion of the aura.

An incarnation on a physical plane is an endurance feat. The process of learning how to handle energy in a physical realm can be compared to the preparation and training for any feat of physical endurance, such as running a marathon. We would not expect someone to attempt to run a marathon with no prior training. Similarly, we would not expect a person to train for a marathon only by running distances of 26.2 miles. Rather, it would be prudent for someone attempting this feat to break the training down into incremental chunks, perhaps starting by walking for a few miles, then jogging, then running, and gradually increasing the distances until, after many, many training sessions, they could run for the full 26.2 miles. The same is true of a physical incarnation. A physical incarnation on earth is a cosmic endurance feat, and the preparation has to be handled in a similar way.

The experiential process in the 3rd dimension begins with the event known as "conception". In the same way that the soul has progressed through the sub-atomic, atomic, molecular, plant and animal realms, each time learning more and more about its state of being and the challenges associated with each realm, a similar process applies to the experience we label as being "human".

The first step for a soul that is new to this dimension is simply to experience the process of conception and very early stages of physical growth (i.e. cell division). Once this phase has been achieved, then the objectives of the soul – for this incarnation – will also have been achieved, and it is no longer necessary to continue with the growth. It is as a result of this outcome that miscarriages are experienced by women.

The next phase of learning is achieved by a soul experiencing a longer development phase as a physical being, but this still only requires a part-term pregnancy. Again, at the end of this slightly longer phase, the objectives of the soul will have been achieved, and the process can be abandoned, again, resulting in a miscarriage, although at a more advanced stage. The third phase of learning is achieved through a soul proceeding all the way through to a full-term pregnancy i.e., achieving full physical development to the point at which it can sustain physical life on its own. At this point, the objectives of the soul will have been achieved, and the soul can return to the realm of spirit having achieved its objectives. The physical outcome of this phase of learning results in the state known as "stillbirth", i.e., the baby has a physical form, but no spiritual force.

When a woman experiences a miscarriage or a baby being stillborn, the physical, psychological and emotional impact can be devastating. From the perspective of spirit, however, it should be noted that there will have been a prior agreement – a **soul Contract** – between the two souls, through which both parties agree to the process, with the soul in the physical realm agreeing to act as the mother (or host) in order to facilitate the development of the other soul, acting in the role of the foetus or baby.

Whilst it can be difficult to come to terms with this, there will have been learning and growth for both parties, and the events experienced will have formed part of the life plan of both souls. Soul contracts are always a win-win for all concerned.

The soul playing the role of the baby will have learned how to multiply cells and how to develop these cells into physical limbs and organs. In the later stages of a pregnancy, it will have learned how to encode the life plan into the subconscious mind, as well as learning how to lay neural pathways in the brain to facilitate the resonance triggers required for a later life, when it chooses to progress that far. For the soul playing the role of the mother, the agreement facilitates a range of physical and emotional experiences associated with pregnancy and the loss of a child.

In all circumstances, the two agendas are in complete accord. This includes situations where the mother, perhaps because of her circumstances at the time, decides to terminate the pregnancy, as well as circumstances where a couple have been trying to have a baby for many months or years. In such circumstances the learning can often relate to guilt, frustration, anger, grief or acceptance.

The next stage of experiential growth occurs when a soul wants to experience physical growth and the birthing process, i.e., to develop to a point at which it can sustain itself in a physical environment outside the womb. When this is the aim, then a soul can choose a path that ends after only a few hours, days, weeks or months – resulting in the experiences we know as "cot–death syndrome", "sudden-infant-death syndrome" or other forms of "child mortality". There are a range of paths designed to facilitate this type of experience, and these include genetic or chromosome disorders, that limit the physical life span of a child, whilst also facilitating a range of experiences for the parents.

The next level of experience occurs when a soul wants to experience being in a physical form, but without fully engaging in the life cycle; it may choose a path that includes the state we label as "disabled", either physically or mentally. This path allows a soul to experience the physical realm in an incremental way.

Another purpose for a disabled path is to facilitate the growth of the other people involved in its life, primarily its parents, siblings or carers, for whom the physical or mental form can facilitate a host of special lessons. Often souls that choose a path which includes a physical or mental disability compensate with increased capabilities in other areas, such as an increased capacity for love, high degrees of patience or some other special skill or teaching.

Whatever the path a soul has chosen to experience, it is necessary to create a separation between the life plan as it has been created in the realm of spirit and the life plan the soul will experience in the physical realm. This is what happens during pregnancy. Once the foetus has reached a state of physical development where the brain is formed, then the soul can begin to encode all the details of the life plan in the subconscious mind. These details include all of the key words and phrases that will resonate with it, as well as the details of key scenes it will experience (later sometimes experienced as "déjà vu").

It would seem reasonable to assume that, if we remembered what we had chosen to experience, we would not approach the experience in the same way. Each event would not hold the same level of potency - it would not be a surprise. It is for this reason that we need a mechanism that helps us to "forget" all the choices we have just made in the realm of spirit, and the forgetting process is the next stage in the Circle of Life.

Chapter 8: The Forgetting Process

Once all the neural pathways have been laid, and all of the choices and elements of the life plan have been transferred into the subconscious mind, it is necessary to "forget" what has been chosen and designed, in order that a soul can encounter each experience as if "new". This forgetting process is known as "drawing the Veils of Maya" (or Veils of Illusion), and can be thought of as placing a lid on the subconscious mind.

The lid that acts as a divide between the conscious and subconscious mind is the ego. This facilitates the fragmentation and separation between the realm of the absolute and the realm of the relative.

We do, however, have a tool that allows us, as physical beings, to penetrate the Veils of Maya, and this tool we call "intuition". In the physical realm, our intuition acts as the link between our conscious and subconscious minds, our purpose and our physical reality, our authentic being and our inauthentic being. Our intuition acts as a conduit linking our physical body with the etheric, emotional, mental, intuitive bodies and our astral body beyond.

As we progress through our physical life, therefore, the more we can learn to listen to and follow our intuition, then the greater the spiritual outcome and the greater the growth for our soul. Intuition is our only link through the Veils of Maya. The closer we are to our path, the more strongly our intuition will resonate – this is our clue that we are on course. Conversely, the more we ignore our intuition, the further we drift from our path.

If only it were that simple! The physical dimension has a very dense energy vibration, and some of the substances we consume (such as drugs, caffeine, alcohol, nicotine sugar and fatty foods) further reduce our capacity to interpret the resonance of our intuition.

The step-down process, required in order to transition from the realm of spirit into the physical realm, happens incrementally during pregnancy. Once in this realm, however, the density of the energy acts as a "gravitational pull" to hold us in this dimension. As a consequence, it is impossible for a physical body to escape from this gravitational pull, and it is also very, very difficult for the human mind to escape mentally from it.

The forgetting process - the building of the layer between the conscious and sub-conscious mind - can take up to two years to complete after the physical birth. This is why babies and small children cannot conceptualise the notion of being separate. For them, initially, they see no distinction between themselves and their mothers or objects in their environment. In the realm from which they have just come, there is no such distinction – there is only the recognition that all is energy, and all is part of the same single whole.

The process of physical development gradually conditions a child to believe that it is separate from its mother, and in time a child will differentiate between the boundaries of itself and those of other people or objects. The similarity of the timing between the forgetting process and the childhood developmental stage known as "the terrible twos" is no coincidence. From a spiritual perspective, when this stage is reached in a child's development, it is ready to embark upon the next stage of its journey – the next stage in the Circle of Life – Conditioning.

Chapter 9: Conditioning

This phase in the Circle of Life can best be summarised by the line from the Talmud:

"Give me the boy until he is seven, and I will give you the man."

Most of our behaviour occurs as a direct result of our conditioning, i.e. what we were taught to believe, accept or fear when we were growing up. There are very few people in the world who have an entirely self-generated belief system. Most of our belief system has been put in place by the early part of our childhood, and the vast majority of it remains unchallenged in our subconscious mind. From a spiritual perspective, however, we need to remember that we have chosen those who will play a key role in our conditioning, and we also know that we have chosen how we wish to be conditioned, (either positively or negatively).

During this phase of an incarnation we initially accept wholesale what our parents, older siblings, extended family or teachers tell us, because we have not yet acquired enough knowledge of our own, and so we defer to other people's understanding of the world. As we grow, this group expands to include friends, lecturers, colleagues, partners, and eventually even our own children and grandchildren.

The purpose of this phase of physical development is to train the mind to believe that certain conditions are true, in order that as we grow into adulthood, we can begin to overturn some of this conditioning as we attempt to grow towards mastery. The timeline for the conditioning phase varies depending upon the individual and the complexity of the life path, but as a general rule there is a sliding scale of impact starting from about the age of two and gradually reducing until the late teens or early twenties – by which time most of us will be capable of "independent" thought.

Conditioning can result in simple beliefs, such as "carrots help you see in the dark", which is a statement often used by parents in an attempt to persuade their children to eat vegetables. The impact of this type of statement is usually easily overcome as we grow older. However, many other more pernicious conditioning statements are much more difficult to overcome, and as a result, can be very destructive. Classic examples of these include: "You are fat", "You are not as pretty as your sister", "You will never amount to anything", "You are too dumb" or "You can't achieve that".

When looked at from the perspective of physical reality, these conditioning statements can only be undone through persistent effort. From the perspective of spirit, however, these same conditioning statements can be seen as opportunities for growth. Remember, we chose our parents or guardians ourselves as well as the life themes we would experience throughout our childhood in order to provide the maximum growth of our soul at this time.

This tends to be the point at which our spiritual destiny gets tricky for most folk. Most of the ideas outlined previously in this book, although perhaps challenging, could be accepted. But, when it comes to the experiences of conditioning, some people feel too overwhelmed by their emotions and reactions to their personal conditioning experience, especially if their conditioning profile included physical, sexual or psychological abuse. The idea that they have actually chosen this experience can be too much.

It can be very difficult to grow beyond such intense experiences. But I would ask those readers affected by such conditioning to consider this idea with an open mind. If you can do so, then it may prove to be a vehicle that will help you transcend the experience itself.

At the level of spirit, all experiences are the same – they are simply physical experiences. There are no "good" or "bad" experiences, for this is a matter of individual perception on the physical plane. This is not to say that those we have chosen to play a key role in our life, such as a parent or guardian, may "forget" and act inappropriately, because this is often the case. Remember that those who play the key roles in our lives are also just learning – and frequently can get it wrong too.

The key point to understand here is that anyone who has experienced abuse in any form has not chosen to be abused. Rather - and this is a critical point - they have chosen to work with another soul to learn about a life theme such as **power** or **control** or **desire**, and it is often the failure of one of the souls to handle the energies associated with the theme of power or control which results in abuse.

When the chosen life path relates to power, there can be two perspectives: "power to" and "power over". If a theme chosen for a life plan relates to learning about "power to", then often circumstances present lessons on having the power to achieve a desired goal. Individuals on this type of path are very often "driven" to succeed in some way, and may trample over others to achieve their goal, thereby failing to learn the lessons about the proper use of power. The process of spirituality, however, is iterative and cyclical, which means that if a soul fails to learn the lessons, irrespective of the role it was playing, then the lessons must be retaken. In this regard it is rather like a universal school system, in which there are many different levels, and a soul can only progress from one level to the next depending upon its ability to achieve a pre-defined standard, i.e. a specific rate of vibration. If a soul cannot achieve the standard, then it cannot progress.

If, after several attempts at a "power to" life theme, a soul is still unable to learn the lessons, then it may decide, with the help of its guide, to experience the opposite of the "power to" theme, which is a "power not to" or a "powerless" theme. In this situation, the soul may then create a life plan in which it adopts the persona of someone who is either physically, mentally or emotionally "powerless", i.e. it gets to experience what it is like on the receiving end of "power to" behaviour. On completion of this life, and after a period of review, the soul may then re-attempt a "power to" theme. The difference this time, however, is that by having experienced the opposite, the soul will hopefully be in a better position to build stronger neural connections between the conscious and the subconscious mind, and thereby increase the possibility of learning the proper use of power.

If the life path a soul has chosen relates to a "power over" theme, then it is often the result of a failure to handle the energy associated with this theme that leads to abuse of power. This can be seen very often in the workplace and in social settings, where people use their position of power in order to try to control others whether through physical, psychological or emotional abuse. All too often with men, it is their failure to control the energy associated with a "power over" path that results in physical, sexual, emotional or psychological abuse, whilst with women, the "power over" path more often results in emotional or psychological abuse.

In the same way as the previous example, a soul that chooses a "power over" theme may have several attempts, via different incarnations, during which he or she will attempt to master this type of energy. And, after several failed attempts, the soul may then decide to create a life plan that enables it to experience the other side of this theme, which is the "powerless" or "victim" theme. If this theme is chosen, then its role in the next incarnation could change from aggressor to that of victim, so that the experiences can be used in future incarnations to build better neural connections, in order that the soul can better learn to control this aspect of power.

Is this to say that every person who has experienced abuse has been an abuser in a previous incarnation? Not necessarily. But (as mentioned previously), a life plan that results in an abuse scenario is often the result of a soul contract which explores issues of power or control or desire. All the events and all the people in our lives are there because we have drawn them there – what we choose to do with them is up to us. Problems never come empty handed. They always bring a gift, and the size of the gift is always greater than the size of the problem – if we can see it that way!

The conditioning profile we experience can be regarded either as a series of obstacles to be overcome or as helping hands from which to obtain leverage. Since the role of conditioning is usually carried out by the parents or guardians, it could be viewed that the role of parents is to set up the challenges for their children, but it is then the role of the children to overcome these challenges, and try not to be like their parents!

Conditioning continues throughout our life, but it generally reduces as we grow older and understand more about the world and how it operates. The more we learn about ourselves the greater the opportunities we find to replace parental, peer and societal conditioning with a self-generated belief system.

The interchange between our conditioning, our physical experiences and our interpretation of these experiences forms a feedback loop (the shaded area in the Circle of Life diagram), that can either operate as a vicious circle or virtuous circle as we attempt to learn to master this experiential cycle. It is this interaction that leads to the next phase in the Circle of Life – growth towards mastery.

Chapter 10: Growth toward Mastery

In the Master Plan that underpins the universe, this is the part of the plan where the rubber meets the road.

By this phase in the Circle of Life a soul has decided upon the themes that are best suited to its growth; chosen the key lessons that relate to each theme; decided where best to place the probability anchor points for its life and underpinned the life plan with resonance energy and synchronistic events. It will have woven these life themes together into a life plan and laid these details within a neural network in the subconscious mind before drawing the Veils of Maya. It will have experienced a step down in energy creating the 6 layers of its body as a conduit for experiential learning; it will have experienced the birthing process; and finally, it will have spent many years accumulating a set of conditioned beliefs, with the help of others whom it has specifically chosen for this purpose. Now it is time to think for itself - to meet the world head on.

The starting point for this phase varies from person to person, but usually it begins when we are old enough to begin to make decisions for our self – probably around the later teenage years. Whereas previously others made decisions on our behalf, and took responsibility for the consequences, now we are able to make our own decisions, and also take full responsibility for the consequences of our own actions.

This phase, therefore, gives us the opportunity to begin to think more deeply about our conditioning. The more we think about our conditioning, the more opportunity we have either to accept that conditioning (and reinforce a pattern of thought or behaviour), or to reject it (and build a new pattern of thought or behaviour). This means that you could potentially experience the same circumstances or events many, many times until you eventually understand why you have drawn these experiences into your life.

This phase is, in effect, a loop that is driven by our conditioning, which in turn drives our belief system that in turn manifests our life experiences. We are what we are, we have what we have and we do what we do, because we think it. For each experience we draw to our self we will have the opportunity to choose how we wish to interpret it – either from a physical or a spiritual perspective. The choice we make leads to this loop acting either as a virtuous circle or a vicious circle.

We make thousands of choices every day. You are reading this particular book, at this moment in time, in this particular place, surrounded by these particular things, and encountering these particular issues in your life as a result of the collective choices you have made in your life to date. Many people believe that they have "no choice", but we always have choices. Each path is only one of many possible paths. These paths are all the same, in that, sooner or later, they all lead back to spirit. Every moment of every day can be seen as a decision point - and each decision point can take you to a new set of experiences. The key question, however, is the context within which you make your choice - are you making a choice in order to grow your soul, or are you making a choice in order to grow your ego?

The Law of Karma

One of the most important universal laws is the law of karma. The law of karma underpins all experiences in this universe. It is the principle of cause and effect or "you reap as you sow". The principle of Karma acts as a "universal balance sheet". On this balance sheet, we can add to our balance with "good" deeds, which build up good karma, or we can subtract from our balance sheet with "bad" deeds, which build up bad karma. If, at the end of our lifetime, we have a surplus of "good deeds" on our balance sheet, then the universe "owes" us. If, however, at the end of our lifetime, we have more "bad deeds" than "good deeds" on our balance sheet, then effectively, we "owe" the universe.

The level of karma associated with each soul reflects the sum total of that soul's thoughts, words and actions throughout ALL of its lifetimes.

The law of karma ensures that there is a balancing of the positive and negative energies associated with each soul, and that ALL the actions of a soul are atoned for as part of the universal process of balance, justice and fairness.

To understand the law of karma is to understand that every thought, word and action will have an impact upon our future experiences. Each of us is responsible for **every** thought, **every** word and **every** action. We can use a simple formula and an example to illustrate how this process works.

In this illustration our level of karmic debt (Kd) is comprised of three elements: Thoughts (T), Words (W) and Actions (A). In order to demonstrate how a karmic balance sheet works, we will allocate a value to each of these variables, which increases with the order of magnitude. Since an action has more significance than a word, we will allocate 3 points to every action. And, similarly, since a word has more significance than a thought, we will allocate 2 points for every word, and 1 point for every thought.

Where the thought, word or action is positive, then these values will be **added** to the karmic balance sheet. But, where the thought, word or action is negative, these values will be **subtracted** from the karmic balance sheet.

In our example (see table 2) we will take a common experience and explore the potential impact of thoughts, words and actions on our karmic balance sheet as we add or subtract points (let's assume that the person in this example has had no previous thoughts before this point, and we will also ignore any karmic points created by anyone else in our example).

Situation: The Tramp	Thought	Word	Action	Karmic Total
I am walking to work one cold morning, when I see a tramp sitting on the side of the pavement. I feel sorry for the guy, and determine that I should ease his plight – at least for today.	+1	-	-	+1
As I walk past him, I reach into my wallet and pull out a £20 note. I give him the money and say "have a good day".	-	+2	+3	+6
As I give the tramp the money, he takes the money without any acknowledgement. I am annoyed by lack of acknowledgement and think "how ungrateful" before walking away.	-1	-	-	+5
I continue on my way to the office and once there, I tell the story of this event to one of my colleagues and imply that the tramp will probably spend the money on alcohol or drugs.	-1	-2	-	+2
At lunch I repeat the story to some of my friends	-1	-2	-	-1
When I get home in the evening. I repeat the same story to my wife.	-1	-2	-	-4

Table 2: Example of Karmic situation

This example is a simple illustration of a complex process, but what we have to remember is that **every** thought, **every** word and **every** action must be accounted for. So, in the process of carrying out what we thought of as a charitable act, we have managed to incur a total of -4 karmic points.

Now try to apply this process to every thought, word and action you have had today. How would your karmic balance sheet look?

The formula for karmic debt can be illustrated as:

Kd = Total Thoughts + Total Words+ Total Actions.

When a soul designs its life plan, it can choose either to "incorporate" karmic debt – in which case, it will receive payback for positive or negative issues within the current lifetime - or it can choose to "accumulate" all the karmic debt associated with each theme, and repay it in another lifetime. If a soul has designed its life plan to incorporate its karmic debt at some time in the future, then, as a result of the actions in our example, it could be that the soul will draw to it an event in which it is desperate for money but is refused because the lender does not believe it will be used responsibly.

As a result of the time delay associated with incorporating karmic debt, it is often very difficult for humans to establish a clear line of sight between the root "cause" of our actions and the "effect" these previous actions have by manifesting the dramas in our current life.

Alternatively, if the soul has chosen to accumulate its karmic debt, then it would carry forward karmic debt into another lifetime, where it would design a range of experiences around the specific theme as part of its next life plan, either through designing a large number of small repayments, or it could be repaid through one big instalment.

Ultimately, the karmic balance sheet requires to be "balanced".

The Law of Karma ensures that individuals who have been responsible for atrocities, or those who are responsible for physical, sexual or psychological abuse in any form, are held to account, and must atone for their actions through subsequent incarnations – thereby ensuring cosmic justice is served.

A common criticism of God or the Source, is that it must in some way be at fault for allowing so much suffering to exist in the world. If the Source is all-knowing and all-powerful and supremely benevolent, then why would it allow all of the suffering in this world to continue?

I believe that this is a matter of perspective. Throughout the universe, I believe that there is order. Our planet is only one of a billion, billion planets within the universe, therefore, I believe that it is inappropriate to judge the events which happen on our planet in isolation. If we had a high enough perspective (a holistic perspective), perhaps then we would be able to see the purpose of each event more clearly. I believe that from this holistic perspective, we would realise that the universe resonates in perfect order, in perfect balance and in perfect harmony.

I also believe that we have to distinguish between "God made" and "man made". Perhaps, from a higher perspective, we could see that whilst the framework was created by the Source, the events that unfold within this framework are primarily created and perpetuated by mankind as a result of failing to learn the lessons set out in our life plan.

Remember that in a relative environment, good and evil are relative concepts, which are created by the existence of universal continuums. In order for the Source to appreciate the state known as supreme benevolence, it had to allow a state known as supreme malevolence, or evil, to also exist. The "good" and the "bad" characters we have known throughout history have been active somewhere along this benevolence continuum, and in this context, we can really only appreciate the kindness and selflessness of a figure such as Mother Teresa, by contrasting her actions to those of a character like Adolf Hitler.

I would also highlight that one of the characteristics of the state of being known as Supreme Benevolence is the capacity to show "unconditional love". The term "unconditional love" is one that often frustrates me, because I believe that it is generally used inappropriately. The state of unconditional love means that there is **NOTHING** that we can do, which would cause the Source to stop loving us. There is NO act for which the

Source would not forgive us. There are no conditions attached to this love. The Source is not judgemental or vengeful, for these states arise out of "conditional" love. The universal law of karma ensures that lessons need to be learned and actions need to be atoned for. It is this understanding which allows us to go with joy amongst the sorrows of the world. The mark of our ignorance is the depth of our belief in injustice and tragedy.

The Akashic Record

Given that spirituality is a process, and also because the human memory is notoriously unreliable and inconsistent, it would make sense to have some mechanism whereby each event or incident of our life could be recorded, in order to assess, at some later stage, whether any growth had been achieved. The universal mechanism used for this recording process is known as the Akashic record.

Akasha is a Sanskrit term that refers to a universal substance upon which is recorded the details of our life. **Every** event, emotion, thought, word or action attributable to us in this lifetime is recorded on our own unique record – our personal Akashic record. As well as holding details of our current life, our personal Akashic record also holds details of our previous incarnations, our previous experiences, reactions, fears, desires, ambitions, successes, failures and any issues that are incomplete, as well as details of any karmic debt we have accrued from previous lives.

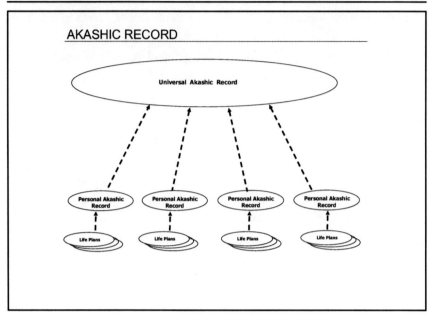

Diagram 13 – The Akashic Record

The Akashic record for each soul is accessed via the intuitive body, which is why if personalities have encountered particularly strong experiences in previous lives the emotional vibration can sometimes "**bleed over**" into its current incarnation and affect its behaviour in its current life.

The phenomenon of "bleed over" can, therefore, be the root cause of many fears and phobias in this lifetime. For example, a person who has a fear of water in this life may have drowned in a previous life, and consequently have a phobia about water that can appear irrational, and that medical specialists may find hard to explain.

"Bleed over" is also the root cause of other human states which science finds hard to explain, such as: **Past Life Recall**, (clearly recalling details from a previous incarnation); and **Déjà vu**, (feelings of having been in the exact situation before as the result of a rehearsal of our life plan when designing in the realm of spirit).

The "growth towards mastery" phase of an incarnation operates as a series of experiential cycles. Whether we experience them as virtuous or vicious circles depends upon how we choose to interpret each experience. If we can transcend our negative conditioning, then we are more likely to experience virtuous circles. If we cannot, however, then we are more likely to experience vicious circles.

Remember that each experience is related to one particular theme, and that we have woven many themes together into our life plan. Remember also that we have carefully designed our own life plan, and will not have given our self more than we can cope with at any one time. Whether we choose to cope with it or not is another matter.

In reality, we will encounter a mixture of both virtuous and vicious circles. We may encounter issues which, no matter how hard we try, we just can't seem to transcend. But there will be other issues with which we are likely to make good progress. Either way, it is this loop - that begins with our own thoughts, that in turn, draws experiences to us, which then allow us to choose how we wish to react – that creates the dramas, or "suffering" in our day-to-day life.

Everyone on earth is currently involved in their own version of these circles. They are different for everyone, and that is what creates the diversity we call life. We each live our lives, day-to-day, moment-to-moment locked into these experiential cycles. Within each moment there is an opportunity to grow towards "Mastery" by overcoming negative conditioning, or conversely, to remain locked into the vicious circles of our life.

As our life progresses, we continually draw events and experiences to us, in order that – through our interpretation of these events and experiences - we can attempt to grow the vibrational level of our soul.

I have outlined two of the main cycles below.

The Material Cycle

The first dynamic – the Material Cycle – is primarily established as a result of how we were conditioned as a child (our conditioning profile). What we were taught as children influences our beliefs in relation to desires and success, and as adults we live our day-to-day lives within the dynamic of this "Material Cycle" (see diagram 14).

In the West, our desire to own material goods is firmly ingrained. As we increase our material **Desire** (reading anti-clockwise from the top of the Material Cycle), we increase our **Thoughts** in relation to these material desires. As we increase our thoughts, we tend to increase our **Actions** in order to manifest these material desires. And, as we increase our actions, we generally increase our level of material "**Success**", as defined by our conditioning and our society. As our own level of success increases, this further fuels our **Desire** for more material goods, thereby completing the loop and starting the Material Cycle all over again.

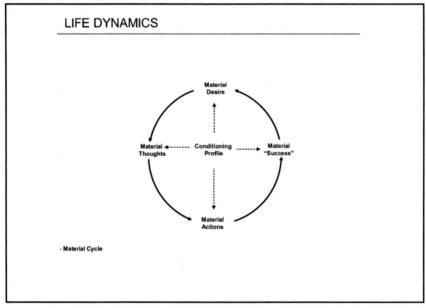

Diagram 14: The Material Cycle

This Material Cycle usually continues operating as a decreasing virtuous circle. As a child we are conditioned to believe that material goods can "appear" in our life just by asking parents or Santa Claus. As we grow older, however, we are further conditioned that "money doesn't grow on trees" and that we can't get everything we want. This pattern continues as a decreasing virtuous circle until roughly between the ages of 35 to 42 because generally, by this point in our life, we will have bought enough "stuff" and should be beginning to recognise that all the "stuff" we have acquired over the years has not made us happy - sometimes even the opposite. Also, by this point, we will be roughly half-way through our life, and as well as having bought enough stuff, we will generally have seen enough people born and enough people die, and tasted enough of life's successes and disappointments to begin to ask ourselves the bigger picture questions, like: **"Is this all there is?"**, **"Why am I here?"**, **"What is the purpose of my life?"** or **"What happens when I die?"**

It is when we reach this stage that the material thoughts, the material actions, and material success - that previously brought us a degree of happiness - tend to begin to feel more and more shallow, and leave us feeling more and more empty; and it is this increasing sense of emptiness with a material life that facilitates the next stage on the journey of spirit – "Searching". It is our increasing frustration with the process of life that acts as a signal to the universe that we are ready to move on. It is precisely this level of frustration with a material life that activates the first stage of the soul - known as the **"Call"** (the stages of the soul are described in detail in the next section). Because our purpose here on earth is not to buy or to accumulate material goods, the Material Cycle, ultimately, will only serve to facilitate a growing sense of emptiness and longing at the core of our being. The **Call** is the universes way of tapping us on the shoulder, and suggesting that we "get on with it!" If we finally listen to the **Call**, it allows us to make the leap from the Material Cycle to the Purpose Cycle.

The Purpose Cycle
The Purpose Cycle operates in opposition to the Material Cycle, but it is only when we put these two sets of dynamics together, as shown in diagram 15 that we begin to appreciate the intricacy of the design.

The gravitational pull of the Purpose Cycle increases as we progress along our lifeline. So, the older we get, the more our satisfaction with material goods tends to decrease, and the more our longing to understand our purpose tends to increase. This is because, as we increase our material success, we also increase our sense of **Emptiness** relating to material goods. And, as our sense of emptiness increases, we increase our **Desire** to know about the purpose of our life. As our desire to understand our purpose increases, so do our **Thoughts** about our purpose.

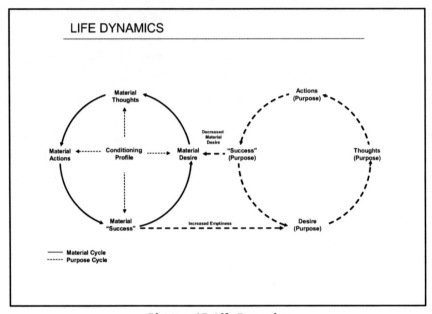

Diagram 15: Life Dynamics

As our thoughts about our purpose increase, this leads to an increase in our **Actions** relating to purpose - typically this will include reading books or attending workshops – i.e. "searching". In turn, with each new book, workshop or conversation our worldview begins to alter. Attitudes and behaviours that were once acceptable to us are now no longer appropriate. The way we view the world and how we interact with it begins to be irrevocably altered. And, as our perspective of life alters, we increase our perception of **Success** in relation to our life Purpose. This feeling of success in relation to beginning to understand our purpose further increases our **Desire** to know more, thereby completing the loop and starting the Purpose Cycle all over again.

The key point in understanding how the Material Cycle leads to searching, is that it increases the level of emptiness we feel in relation to material goods and it is this emptiness that (eventually) acts as a sling-shot mechanism to catapult us from the material trajectory to a spiritual trajectory. The greater our sense of emptiness, the higher the probability that we will make the leap from the Material Cycle to the Purpose Cycle.

Generally, the first half of our life is focused on materialistic experiences (as defined in the "Material Cycle"), and the second half on spiritual exploration, (as defined by the "Purpose Cycle").

If we choose to grow towards mastery, then we can expect our growth to be categorised into 6 phases – the six stages of the soul.

The Six stages of the soul
The six stages of the soul are detailed as follows:

1. The Call
The first stage of the soul is known as the **Call.**

The **Call** usually comes when the person understands enough about "life" to begin to question the meaning of life, and this typically occurs between the ages of 35 and 42. Although The Call is persistent throughout our life, unfortunately, due to the level of "noise" in our busy lives, many people never hear it, let alone heed it, and consequently, a large portion of humanity remains locked in the vicious material cycle, becoming more and more attached to their material possessions, and consequently, more and more empty inside.

The Call, however, remains persistent. It will try endlessly throughout our lifetime, but it is only if we choose to hear it that we can move on to the next stage. For those who do heed the Call and begin to question their lives, the questioning increases the sense of longing which, in turn, generally leads to a sense of frustration with the world. And it is precisely this sense of frustration with our pursuit of materialism and our conditioned nature that acts as the catalyst to search for meaning.

2. The Search

Once we heed the Call, then the **Search** stage begins to alter the course of our life. During this phase, we search for meaning, purpose and authenticity. Common characteristics of this stage include feeling "drawn" to alternative books, feeling inclined to attend workshops on spirituality, or workshops that offer a different perspective on life, or generally, just pursuing lines of enquiry that resonate with us. All of these activities lead to growth in our level of knowledge. This stage may take some time - sometimes even years of researching and exploring spiritual perspectives, before we finally arrive at a path that resonates with us.

Some people never make it through this phase, however. We sometimes get caught up in a "knowledge loop", where our pursuit of knowledge overtakes the pursuit of purpose and growth, and we live a life of believing that we do not have enough information, and need to read "just one more book" or attend "just one more workshop".

At some point, however, we do find something that feels like our purpose, and it is at this stage that the Search gives way to the **Struggle**.

3. The Struggle

There is a line in the Koran that says;

"If you say you believe, do you think you won't be tested?"

I think this sentiment best sums up this stage of the soul.

For most people, the **Struggle** is the most frustrating stage of their development. Once the Call has been heeded, and the Search has been negotiated, then a dilemma is created. On the one hand, we have this new information about the journey of spirit and the illusions of this dimension. But, on the other hand, we are firmly tied into these illusions via our current responsibilities as a husband, wife, partner, father, mother, friend or employee.

The primary characteristic of this stage is an internal struggle with our own self, as we try to reconcile a spiritual perspective with a lifestyle in a material world. As the Struggle stage continues, all areas of our life are questioned. How do I want to live my life? Where do I want to live my life? With whom do I want to live my life? How do I want to earn my living?

This stage is designed to test us to the extreme. The struggle can sap the energy from us, as two worldviews compete for our attention. This happens as a result of the ego. In order for us to fully embrace a spiritual path, the ego needs to be broken. The ego, however, will not let go lightly – since it's key function relates to defining the personality through the job we do, where we live and the things we have.

The further we progress through this stage, the greater our desire to follow a spiritual path, then the more the ego fights to keep control and the greater the challenges we will face in our life. The challenges have many faces: debts, illness, redundancy, rejection, depression and the breakdown of relationships are common trials during this stage. For many, the struggle is just too great. The confusion and uncertainty about a spiritual path, generally combined with a personal life which is fast turning into a train wreck, can prove to be too much – and most people abandon their spiritual journey during this stage.

It is, however, only the act of persevering through these trials that allows us to claim our place on the spiritual high ground.

4. The Scream
For those who do have the stamina to persevere with the struggle, there comes a point at which their frustrations, confusion and anger with the universe, all boil over, which results in the **Scream**.

There will be many, many occasions during the Struggle in which a soul will feel confused and disorientated in relation to its spiritual journey. In fact, the Struggle and the Scream stages act as an upward spiral that feed off each other. The further a soul journeys, the more frustrated it becomes, and the more frustrated it becomes, the more often it screams. This continues in a cyclical way, all the while testing the resolve of the individual soul.

Legend has it that King Solomon asked the royal jeweller to make him a ring and inscribe on the ring a phrase that would remain true in all circumstances. The inscription on the ring presented to King Solomon read "**This too will change**". I have found this phrase very useful during my own journey. For although we cannot always see the path clearly - often the path is blocked with metaphysical obstacles – we can be assured that "this too will change", and when it does, our path will be clear, and we will once again be able to continue with our journey. We will be able to (as Rudyard Kipling suggests in his poem "If") "meet with triumph and disaster, and treat these two impostors just the same".

Ultimately, the Scream acts as a signal from us to the universe that enough is enough. It is a challenge to the universe to either "put up, or shut up". It is the signal the universe is looking for in order to facilitate the next stage of the soul – the **Breakthrough**.

5. The Breakthrough

The **Breakthrough** generally comes a few steps beyond our ultimate "give up" point. This phenomenon is well documented in the material world. It is only when we have all but given up, and then make "one last attempt", that our persistence and perseverance is rewarded by a breakthrough of some kind. The process of spirituality is no different.

The nature of any breakthrough tends to be specific to an individual. For a small number this breakthrough could be "enlightenment"; more often, however, it is likely to take the form of a new relationship, or a new job or a synchronistic meeting. Whatever the context of the breakthrough, the result is unmistakable – progress!

The breakthrough provides hope for our soul. It provides a degree of peace for our soul after the trials and tribulations of the previous stage. The breakthrough is not the end of our journey, however. Very often the breakthrough simply leads to new questions, and facilitates a new Search, albeit at a more evolved level.

It is only when we have fully satisfied our self with our questioning that we experience the final Breakthrough, which leads to the Return.

6. The Return

Once we have achieved our final Breakthrough, there is still the matter of living the rest of our life. The adapted Zen saying:

"First comes laundry, then comes enlightenment, then comes laundry"

is apt for this stage.

This stage is about the application of all of our learning from our journey so far, to the rest of our journey.

The six stages of the soul are outlined in diagram 16.

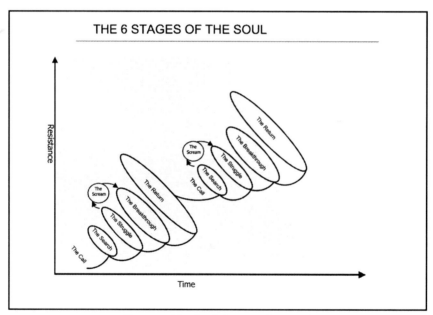

Diagram 16: The 6 Stages of the soul

After a time – sometimes a short time, sometimes a long time – a soul will have planned to leave this physical realm. When it gets to this point, it is ready to enter the next phase on the Circle of Life – the Transition.

Chapter 11: Transition

The Transition phase includes the process we label as "Death".

In the same way a soul chooses its date, time and place of birth, I believe that it also chooses its date, time and place of death.

The physical body is simply a vehicle the soul uses in order to access experiences on a physical plane. Once our experiences have been completed, there is no longer any requirement for a physical body. It is rather like wearing a wet-suit and aqua lung in order to go diving. Once we have completed our dive, there is no need to continue to wear the wet-suit and aqua lung, and so we discard them.

When we entered the physical realm, it was necessary to undergo a "step-down" in energy vibration. When we want to leave the physical realm and re-enter the realm of spirit, the opposite is the case – we need to undergo a "step-up" in the rate of vibration of our energy.

The Step Up Process
It is often reported, by those who have had a "near death experience" that they have seen a tunnel with a bright light at the end, and they also experience a sensation of being "drawn" towards the light.

This is because when a soul undergoes the "step-down" process, it effectively creates a tunnel connecting the spiritual realm with the physical realm, with each body progressively acting as an energy transformer that moves the soul further away from the Source with each degree of separation. When we die, the step-down process is reversed and the soul turns back towards the Light, which can be seen resonating through the other layers of the body. This process is outlined in diagram 11.

The transition process (of which the step-up process is only part) can be disorientating. It is common for a soul, especially a "new soul" - a soul that has not had many incarnations into this dimension - to be confused by this change in energy state. It is for this reason that the soul is very often greeted by a familiar face from their most recent incarnation in the physical realm when they first make the transition. This could be a mother or father, a friend, a relative, or even a sporting hero. The key characteristic of a "greeter" is that it will be someone that we would trust and believe.

It is the responsibility of the entity that greets a newly transitioned soul to help them initially re-orient into this new state of being. After a period of adjustment, the newly transitioned soul will then rejoin their soul Group, which is likely to include those souls who played the role of father, mother, son or daughter. Alternatively, a newly transitioned soul may decide to take some time alone for peaceful reflection upon the life just ended before they progress to the next stage which reviews their most recent incarnation in detail.

"Old souls" – souls who have incarnated many times before - will have made this journey many times before, and will be familiar with the process and it is more likely that they would simply choose to return directly to their soul Group. Members of our Soul Group will feel very familiar to us, and once we return, we can enjoy a period of rest and recuperation, which we need because any experience of the physical realm can be exhausting and deplete our spiritual energy.

Whilst from a human perspective, we may consider the elapsed time of an incarnation on Earth a long time (on average 70+ years); from the perspective of spirit (since the notion of time operates in a very different way in the realm of spirit) it appears a very short time – perhaps about the equivalent of 20 minutes of Earth time. So, when a soul departs from the realm of spirit to experience a "lifetime" on Earth, for those awaiting its return it actually feels as though they have just popped out for 20 minutes, and not like they will be gone for 70 years.

Whichever way a soul chooses to re-orientate itself with the spiritual realm, after a while the soul will want to turn its attention back to learning and growth. When this time comes, the soul will be joined by its guide or guides and the journey of the soul continues with the next stage in the Circle of Life - The Life Review.

Chapter 12: The Life Review

The Life Review phase is exactly as it suggests. During this phase a soul will work with its guide, and sometimes other members of its soul Group, to review each moment of the life it has just lived. With its guide, the soul will consider what it set out to achieve during its most recent incarnation – its target experiences. If, for example, the soul set out to experience "triumph over adversity", then did it actually manage to achieve this? If not, then where did things go wrong?

The review of an incarnation is only possible because every moment in the life of the soul will have been recorded on its personal Akashic record. Every situation and event, as well as every emotion associated with each event, is also recorded, not only for the soul, but also for all the other souls involved in each event. This means that, as a soul reviews each situation or event that occurred during its life, it can not only re-live how it felt, but it can also feel how the other people involved in the situation felt. So, if in one situation, the soul was abusing its power by shouting at others, it will have a chance to review the circumstances that led to this event from a higher perspective – a more holistic perspective. This higher perspective facilitates a greater understanding of the situation. As well as experiencing and understanding the emotion felt, the soul will also be able to experience how the others felt – perhaps their fear, or their remorse, or their anger – and the soul will also be able to see the ramifications of its actions, as others further perpetuate the negative energy instigated by the soul. The same, of course, is true of any positive actions originated by this soul.

This stage is not a judgement, as portrayed in some religious texts. It is not the actions of the soul being judged by guides or by the Source, but rather, it is only the soul itself that decides, from a place of total honesty and holistic understanding, whether the lessons set out were learned or not. If the soul has achieved the outcome it set out to achieve, then there is no need to repeat the lesson. If, however, it did not, then it can decide to have another attempt at the same lesson, or attempt the lesson in a slightly different way, in a different incarnation.

The lessons that remain on a soul's list – either because it did not successfully complete them in its last incarnation, or because it has yet to experience them – act as inputs into the design of its next incarnation, its next set of target experiences, and so the Circle of Life begins again.

In the first part of this book, we have explored the process of spirituality, and examined how this process works.

The nature of life in the physical realm, however, is such that even the most strong-willed and determined can be blown off course every now and then. When this happens, life becomes a navigation issue, and in order to navigate well, we need to have good tools.

Even though the details of our life plan are locked into our sub-conscious mind with the Veils of Maya drawn over them, there are ways in which we can understand more about the paths we have chosen.

In part 2, therefore, I will outline some tools and techniques which I have found useful in helping me understand my journey and the life plan choices that I have made.

Part 2 - Navigation Tools

Chapter 13: The Pythagorean Triangle

The Pythagorean triangle is a metaphysical divination tool, which uses a number system in order to unlock some of the encoded details of the life plan a soul has chosen, thereby facilitating a greater understanding and interpretation of the life path set out for the personality. Despite the fact that the use of numbers as a divination tool can be traced back many thousands of years to the ancient cultures of Babylonia, China, India and Egypt, it is Pythagoras, the Greek philosopher, mathematician and mystic, who is credited with first consolidating the various approaches into a single system, around the 6th century BC.

Pythagoras believed that each planet in the solar system vibrated at a unique frequency, which resonated with the harmony of the universe. These cosmic vibrations he called "the Music of the Spheres". He also believed that everything in the universe vibrated at its own special harmony, and that the higher the rate of vibration, the more "spirit force" it contained, and the more positive its nature. But the converse was also true, in that, the lower the rate of vibration, the less "spirit force" it contained, and the more negative its nature.

He believed that nature is a set of mathematical relationships which is described through numbers. He called this "Sacred Geometry" – and it was from his study of this sacred geometry that he developed the "science of names and numbers", which studies the significance of names and numbers in relation to human conditioning and experience.

In his esoteric and mystical schools, he taught the spiritual view that the date of birth and the birth name hold the key to understanding a life plan, since these contain a detailed portrait of the personality, its chosen purpose, its potential, its challenges and the cycles of its life. By understanding this sacred geometry, he believed, the personality could also better understand the psychological conditioning around it. His sacred geometry system - more commonly referred to today as "Numerology" - links the nine primary universal energy forces to the arithmetical numbers we use today (1 to 9), and reduces all names and numbers down to a number between 1 and 9. There is a lot of information that can be distilled from a date of birth and a birth name but, for the sake of simplicity, I will highlight only a few of these, and I would suggest that there are many good books on numerology available in most bookstores for those readers who are interested in exploring this topic further.

The Pythagorean Triangle - or holy Tetraktys - uses the date of birth to describe the creative interplay of energies present in each person's life. An example of a Pythagorean Triangle for someone with a date of birth of 24/8/1962 is shown in diagram 17.

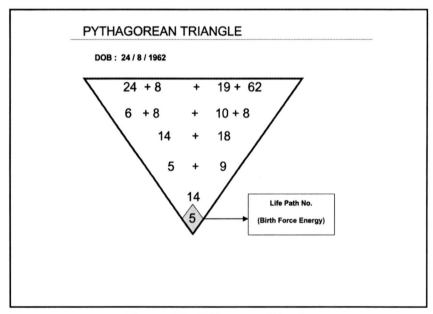

Diagram 17 – Pythagorean Triangle

The Pythagorean Triangle, uses a "Reduction" method to calculate life path details. Using this method, each part of our date of birth is reduced to number between 1 and 9 by a process of repeated addition. In this case, the day of birth is the 24th – which means that we add together each integer (2+4), to give the number 6 on the line below. Next we look at the month of birth which is the 8th. Since this is already a single integer between 1 and 9, we need not reduce any further. Finally we turn to the year of birth 1962. We reduce the century down separately from the decade and year component, before re-joining these two components in the next stage of the process. By adding the 1 and the 9 of the century we get 10. In a similar way, by adding the 6 and the 2 of the decade and year, we get the number 8.

Our first line of reduction therefore, gives us 6 + 8 + 10 + 8, which now need to be reduced further. By adding the 6 and the 8 from the day and month, we obtain the number 14, and by adding the 10 and the 8 from the century and the decade and year, we obtain the number 18.

On the second line of our reduction we continue the same process. By taking the number 14 and adding the 1 and the 4 together, we obtain the number 5, and by taking the number 18 and adding the 1 and the 8, we obtain the number 9.

We can now add the third line of our reduction (5+9), to obtain the number 14, and we can then reduce this number by adding the 1 and the 4 to give us our Life Path Number, which in this case, is the number 5.

Whilst the life path number (in our example 5) is the most significant number for understanding a person's life path, the double digit number which immediately precedes the life path number is also important (in our example 1 and 4), and it is for this reason that when expressing a life path all three numbers are usually written together - in our example the life path would be written as 14/5.

Whilst the number to the right of the slash highlights the "**primary issues**" relating to our life path, the two digits to the left of the slash are also important, because they highlight the "**component issues**" which relate to our life path.

Where the life path number provides the main context and backdrop for life issues, the component issues will generally provide many of the themes for the day-to-day dramas that play out in our life.

There are different numerological methods that can be used to calculate a life path number. The three most common calculation methods are the "Reduction Method" (shown above), the "Adding Across" method and the "Adding Down" method.

In the "Adding Across" method, each integer in the string is simply added together to give an overall total, that is then reduced to a number between 1 and 9 - e.g. if we use the adding across method for our previous example the result is as follows: 2+4+8+1+9+6+2 = 32; 3+2=5, (that gives a life path number of 32/5).

With the "Adding Down" method, the elements of the date are arranged in columns before the columns are added together as follows:

$$
\begin{array}{r}
1962 \\
8 \\
{}^{1}24 \\
\hline
1994 \\
\hline
\end{array}
$$

The digits from the resulting number (1994) are then added together (1+9+9+4) to arrive at the final life path number of 23/5.

Whilst the resultant life path number should be the same, irrespective of the calculation method used, the component numbers could be different. In our example, the full life path number using the "reduction" method would be 14/5. When using the "adding across" method, however, the full life path number would be 32/5, and when using the "adding down" method, the life path number would be 23/5 and this can lead to inconsistent interpretations.

There is no question that a method which simply adds the numbers straight across, before then reducing is the most simple. I, however, prefer to use the reduction method of the Pythagorean triangle for two main reasons.

Firstly, I believe this method provides more consistent and accurate analysis, and secondly, because this method highlights the occurrence of specific number patterns that can indicate energy influences or karmic debt patterns.

In a previous chapter I outlined the role of karma in obtaining universal balance. The way that karmic debt or karmic lessons show up as part of a life path is through the presence of the number patterns: 10, 13, 14, 16 or 19 as part of the reduction process, or as a component part of the life path number. When these numbers arise as part of a reduction process, then it indicates that the personality is carrying some karmic issues into this life. This means that this lifetime will probably have increased challenges with respect to the particular karmic themes, as outlined below.

10 = New Start (Karmic Completion)

The number 10 relates to karmic completion. A 10 usually indicates that there has been a past misuse of personal power, and that we are now called to use courage, independence, and leadership to bring about a new beginning. This means that we will encounter situations and people in this lifetime that will allow us to complete the karma present in those situations. 10 is generally considered a fortunate number and can allude to triumph if difficult situations are faced up to.

Karmic Life Paths = 10/1, 28/10, 37/10 or 46/10

Until the lessons are understood, a personality on this life path will often manifest the negative side of a life path of 1, which include: being aggressive, opinionated, egotistical, pushy, wilful and a know-it-all.

13 = Lessons on Work

The number 13 relates to hard work in all areas of our life. The 13 indicates that in previous incarnations we have not taken our fair share of the load, but rather, have expected others to carry us in some form. It can also indicate an abuse with words, (gossiping or manipulating others through the use of words). Whilst this number indicates a growing spiritual consciousness, it is likely that we will face many obstacles which will force us to deal with issues relating to matters of expression and discipline.

Karmic Life Path = 13/4

Until the lessons are understood, a person on this path will often manifest the negative side of a life path of 4, which include: insecurity, suspicion, repression, stubbornness and joylessness.

14 = Lesson on Freedom

The number 14 relates to past issues with freedom. The number 14 suggest that in some way we have misused, avoided or misunderstood freedom in past lives, and now in this life we are meant to bring the freedom issue into balance. With a 14 showing as part of our life path, this highlights past lifetimes where freedom was abused. The debt is to re-learn the value of freedom and the discipline required to earn this freedom. In a past life, those with this number may have found freedom for themselves at the expense of others, and that's where the debt comes in – there was some kind of irresponsibility and lack of accountability in the past.

Karmic Life Path = 14/5

Until the lessons are understood, a person on this path will often manifest the negative side of a life path of 5, which include: impatience, impulsiveness, being lustful, moody, addicted, discontent, conceited and restless.

16 = Lessons of Love:

When a 16 is highlighted as an embedded karmic number within a date of birth it highlights that there has been an abuse of love in previous lifetimes. The 16 can arise from past involvement in illicit love affairs, lack of integrity with the feeling of others regarding love, family or commitment that caused suffering to others: in some manner, love was abused.

Karmic Life Path = 16/7

Until the lessons are understood, a person on this path will often manifest the negative side of a life path of 7, which include: aloofness, being moody, dreamy, cynical, loner, suspicious, unsympathetic and critical.

19= Lesson on Power

The karmic debt of this number stems from past abuses of power. Abuse of acting in a completely self-centred manner, blind to everything except self-fulfilment of one's own desires. The karmic lessons on this path relate to the proper use of power and also learning to stand on our own. This path could include many lessons through which we will be forced to stand up for our self, or alternatively, feel as though we are standing alone. The purpose of this path is to teach independence, consideration for others, and having to assert our self.

Karmic Life Path = 19/1

Until the lessons are understood, a person on this path will often manifest the negative side of a life path of 1, which include: selfishness, intimidation, dependence, egotism, laziness and aggression.

Diagram 18 highlights how the Pythagorean triangle method allows us to uncover karmic numbers, which may have remained hidden if using other calculation methods.

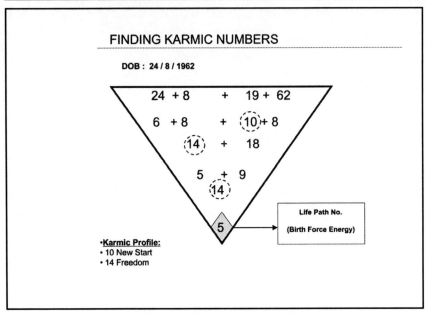

Diagram 18: Finding Karmic Numbers

In addition to the numbers 1 – 9, most numerological systems also use the numbers 11, 22, 33 up to and including 99, which are deemed to be "Master Numbers".

The best way to describe a "Master Number" is to think of the keyboard on a piano. On the metaphysical piano the numbers 1 through 9 would represent the first nine keys, whilst the life path numbers 11 through 99 would be the same "notes" but an octave higher i.e. the master numbers are of a higher vibration than the life path numbers 1 through 9.

This does not mean that a master number life path is "better", it simply means that there is more birth force energy associated with these numbers, and can, consequently, mean that the lessons associated with such paths can be more intense.

Only a very limited number of life paths relate to "Master Numbers". In order to determine if our life path is one of these paths, then the result of the calculation process (reduction, adding across or adding down) must equal either 11 or 22 or 33 etc when using at least two out of the three calculation methods outlined above.

Now it's your turn to find out more about your own life path. Use a blank sheet of paper, draw triangle and work out your own life path number.

Once you have determined your single number (between 1 and 9), then you can begin to relate this to the characteristics of a Life Path. I have included a summary description of each life path and the issues and lessons associated with that path in appendix 1 at the back of this book. Remember to also check the descriptions of your component numbers, since this will add more detail.

The 9 primary life path themes are outlined in table 3:

Life Path Number	Theme
1	Creativity & Confidence
2	Co-operation and Balance
3	Expression & Sensitivity
4	Stability & Process
5	Freedom & Discipline
6	Vision & Acceptance
7	Trust & Openness
8	Power & Abundance
9	Integrity & Wisdom

Table 3: The 9 primary life themes

In our example above, therefore, a person with a date of birth of 24/8/1962 would have a life path of 5, which means they would have chosen to experience issues under the broad theme of "Freedom & Discipline" i.e. learning how to find inner freedom through the development of discipline in their life. Much of the drama, tension or conflict in this persons life, therefore, will come from their failure to develop or maintain a disciplined approach to their life, which will lead to feelings of being trapped and will tend to fuel a need to "escape".

Further detail relating to this particular life path can be obtained by also considering the component numbers that were a 1 and a 4. The significance of these two numbers is that issues associated with the 1 and the 4 will consistently be encountered along the path. So, whilst the overall life path deals with issues relating to "Freedom & Discipline", the person on this path will firstly have to encounter issues relating to the number 1 energy (Creativity & Confidence), and also the number 4 energy (Stability & Process).

Using the Pythagorean triangle reduction method has also highlighted that our example life path of 14/5 is actually a karmic life path. This means that the person on this path is likely to have a harder time because they are attempting to pay off some karmic debt during this lifetime.

Most people who complete a triangle believe that the numbers represent a very accurate reflection of their life and their life issues, and hence, the path they are currently on, and they believe that this method does provide excellent insight into why they experience the events and circumstances which continually recur in their life.

A small percentage of people, however, do not see any relevance between the path number that they have calculated from their date of birth, and the summary detail of the path, provided in the appendix. Over the years, I have found that this is typically down to one of three possible reasons:

1. It is very common to find people make simple errors in their addition, and then end up reading about the wrong path! So re-check your arithmetic, or ask someone else to check it for you.
2. Another common error is that the date of birth will have been written incorrectly. The most common failing here is that we use the abbreviated century when reducing the date e.g. rather than write 1962, we write this as 62, thereby missing the 19 from the front.
3. The final reason tends to be because we do not see our self as this type of person. When this is the situation, then check with friends, family and colleagues. It is very common in this situation for others to see us differently than we see our self. If we take a closer look, then it will be possible to see how our current characteristics and personality traits actually do reflect the path we are on.

Chapter 14: Birth Name Triangle

As part of its life plan, a soul will have chosen its birth name and agreed this name with those entities that will play the role of its parents. This is why one particular name (or set of names), will have resonated more clearly with our parents than any other.

Encoded within our birth name are details about the challenges we have set for our self, as well as details of the personality of the character we have chosen to play. Our birth name can be distilled to reveal many interesting details relating to our current life. The most useful number I have found, however, is the **Destiny** number.

The Destiny Number

This number is distilled using all the letters of our birth name, and it reveals our overall purpose for this life i.e. the direction and context within which we will be most successful.

The distillation process for names is quite straightforward. All letters in your birth name can be converted to a number between 1 and 9 by looking up the letter using the following table, and then assigning the numeric value at the top of the column.

1	2	3	4	5	6	7	8	9
A	B	C	D	E	F	G	H	I
J	K	L	M	N	O	P	Q	R
S	T	U	V	W	X	Y	Z	-

Using the table above, we can see that the letter "A" has a value of 1, whilst the letter "N" has a value of 5, "Z" has a value of 8 and so on.

In order to determine a numeric value for your birth name, therefore, you simply need to convert the letters in your birth name (i.e. your name as stated on your birth certificate), into a numeric string using the above table.

As an example, let's say your birth certificate shows the name "Thomas John Walker": the method for determining the destiny number is outlined in diagram 19.

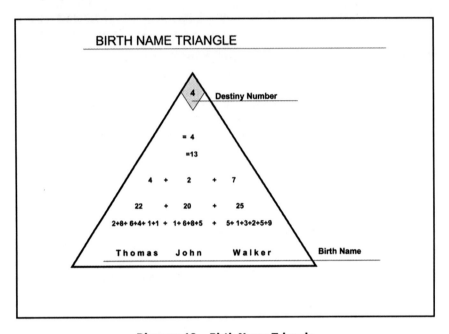

Diagram 19 – Birth Name Triangle

In this case, with a destiny number of 4, then the direction for this persons' life relates to the life theme of "Stability & Process". Success in this lifetime will, therefore, be determined by the degree to which this person is prepared to work hard on practical issues.

Table 4 below provides a brief summary of each destiny number.

Number	Destiny Themes / Issues
1	Leadership, Independence, Courage, Innovation, Confidence
2	Co-operation, Balance, Harmony, Patience, Relationships
3	Communication, Expression, Creativity, Inspiration, Encouragement
4	Building, Practicality, Hard Work, Process, Stability, Order
5	Freedom, Discipline, Curiosity, Adaptability, Change
6	Family, Service, Nurturing, Home, Community, Harmony
7	Research, Analysis, Contemplation, Perfectionism, Inner Wisdom
8	Achievement, Success, Recognition, Business, Organisation, Power
9	Sensitivity, Healing, Love, Integrity, Tolerance, Forgiveness
11	Creativity, Inspiration, Illumination, Intuition, Transform lives of others
22	Build projects for benefit of mankind, Build using spiritual principles
33	Loving Service, Demonstrate a higher consciousness of love

Table 4 – Destiny Number Themes

The key point to remember here is that it is your name, as it appears on your birth certificate, which is the key element in understanding your destiny. If you were adopted, changed your name or now use a different spelling of your name, then this does alter your original energy profile, but only acts as a secondary energy profile. To establish a complete picture, therefore, you must access the details as they are presented on your birth certificate to gain the relevant information, because this highlights your original energy profile.

Individual Names

When considering the total impact of your birth name, as well as considering the composition of letters, each name should be considered individually, since this provides extra insights into your life plan.

The number associated with your first name highlights the personal lessons you have chosen, as well as your physical and mental abilities. The number(s) associated with your second name (or names), highlights your hidden abilities (the good and the bad), as well as your emotional profile, and the number associated with your surname highlights the characteristics you have inherited from your family, as well as your spiritual nature.

Because your first name highlights the lessons you have chosen to learn in this lifetime in order to grow your soul, the number distilled from your first name is known as your "**Growth**" number. In the example above, the first name of "Thomas" has a value of 4 which highlights that growth for this personality will be pursued through experiences relating to the number 4 - Stability & Process – and this is further compounded by having 4 as the overall Destiny number, and having a 4 as a life plan component number.

The middle name "John" reveals details of his emotional character as well as his hidden abilities. In this case, the number 2 highlights that when it comes to his emotions and abilities, the key characteristic will be "Co-operation and Balance". This indicates that this person has ability to be persuasive, supportive, considerate and adaptable on the one hand. But, on the other hand, they can quickly become over co-operative and then over emotional, needy, moody and even underhand.

The family name of "Walker" has a vibrational profile of 7, which equates to the life theme of "Trust & Openness". Under this profile the person would have a desire for knowledge, study, analysis and learning as well as an understanding of spirit. There is also likely to be a strong desire for privacy, as well as experiences relating to trust for all personalities associated with this family.

Vibrational Profile Chart

A "Vibrational Profile Chart" is created by two interlocking triangles. The Pythagorean triangle, pointing downward, represents our chosen life path, as encoded in our date of birth, and this triangle interlocks with our Birth Name triangle pointing upwards, that represents our life plan challenges as encoded through our birth name. An example of this is highlighted in diagram 20.

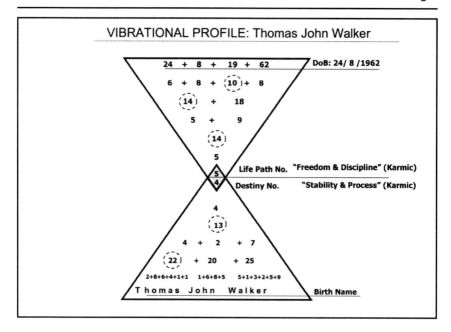

VIBRATIONAL PROFILE: Thomas John Walker

DoB: 24/ 8 /1962

24 + 8 + 19 + 62

6 + 8 + (10) + 8

(14) + 18

5 + 9

(14)

5

5
4

4

(13)

4 + 2 + 7

(22) + 20 + 25

2+8+6+4+1+1   1+6+8+5   5+1+3+2+5+9

Thomas John Walker

Life Path No.   "Freedom & Discipline" (Karmic)

Destiny No.   "Stability & Process" (Karmic)

Birth Name

Diagram 20 – Vibrational Profile Chart

When we use the life path number we calculated earlier for the date of birth 24/8/1962, which was 5, and consider this with the birth name number of 4, then this indicates that the personality of Thomas John Walker will continually experience issues relating to his life path number of 5 - Freedom & Discipline – until he learns to develop a consistent set of processes, i.e. developing a consistent set of processes in the key areas of his life will bring stability. To maintain this stability, however, these processes have to be underpinned by a discipline which ensures a consistent adherence to these processes. If this can be achieved, the "freedom" that is sought in this lifetime could be achieved.

During his lifetime, Thomas John Walker is likely to face issues of greater intensity because both his life path and the destiny number relate to karmic issues that will have to be dealt with in this lifetime.

His growth number (derived from the value of his first name of Thomas), however, is a master number, which suggests that there is increased potential in this lifetime.

Chapter 15: Joint Life Paths

The purpose of our life here on Earth is to grow the rate of vibration of our own soul, and the mechanisms to achieve this come via the lessons presented to us through the life themes we have chosen.

Since no man is an island, our life here on Earth necessitates a degree of interaction with others through relationships of some kind. Relationships come in many shapes and forms: families, friendships, colleagues or acquaintances to name but a few, and each relationship can have many different attributes: positive, negative, victim, persecutor, loving, taking, sharing and so on.

The important point to remember is that, at its base level, every relationship forms part of a joint path. Irrespective of the context for the relationships, each can be distilled down into joint paths. Within a family setting, for example, we have a relationship with our husband, wife or partner. But we also have separate relationships with each of our children. This means that a family of four people, comprises 6 different relationship sets: 1. husband and wife, 2. husband and 1st child, 3. husband and 2nd child, 4. wife and 1st child, 5. wife and 2nd child and 6. 1st child and 2nd child. The dynamics of relationships become even more complicated within larger social groups or within a work context, where there may be literally hundreds of different relationship sets.

Everything in the universe is underpinned by energy, and relationships are no different – we are energy beings in an energy universe. This means that the interactions we have with each other through our relationships can be thought of as "a point where two energy profiles collide". I have found that the best way to look at relationships is to consider them like waves on an ocean.

In situations where two waves collide, where a peak meets a peak, then there will be a positive amplification of the energy – i.e. we will probably get on very well with the other person. However, in situations where a trough meets a trough, there will be a negative amplification of the energy, and this type of relationship could very well end up in conflict. In a situation where a peak meets a trough, then there will be a cancelling out of energies, and we will probably not feel strongly about the other person one way or the other. Each of us has peak, trough or null relationships in our life.

When considering our relationship with another person, it is important that we firstly understand about our own life path and the challenges that we have set for our self – for it is in response to these challenges that other people have been drawn into our life. The challenges we are presented with never come empty handed – they always bring gifts. In my experience, the size of the gift is always greater than the size of the challenge, that is, if we can rise above our conditioned response to these situations and experiences and try to take a spiritual perspective of each of the challenges we are presented with.

Over the years, as my understanding of my own life path has increased, I have tried to maintain a two step process when presented with challenges.

Step 1: Identify what is happening
Ask yourself "what's happening here?" When a situation arises; try to pause for a moment and ascertain what is actually happening. Run through the details in your mind paying particular attention the topic or theme, the personalities, the place, the time and so on.

Step 2: Identify why it's happening
Ask yourself "why is this happening?" Consider the context for your life path and the key learning themes you have set out for yourself – then try to review what has happened against this framework.

If, for example, you are being shouted at by your boss, your analysis of

what is happening may look like this:

- Office setting in front of colleagues
- Boss being aggressive
- Over reacting to a work situation
- Everyone looking on
- This is the 4th time in the last 2 weeks
- I feel humiliated and upset

When you consider the **why** aspect, it may look like this:

- Life path relates to "confidence" and "expression"
- This could be an opportunity to stand up for myself
- Could be an opportunity to find my own voice and respond
- Could be an opportunity to teach my boss about "respect"

The more often you can ask these questions, the more you are able to obtain a different perspective on situations and the lessons they present for us. Remember, challenges never come empty handed.

Initially you may find it difficult to achieve this type of analysis "in the moment". In time and with continued practice, however, you will learn to ask these questions as the situation is developing and thereby eventually gain mastery over the situation.

In my best moments, I can remember to ask myself these questions as the experience is unfolding before me. On other occasions, however, I try to answer these questions only after having been sucked in by the experience – but, better late than never, I suppose.

I have found that the collision points in relationships can generally be understood better by comparing and contrasting two key numbers;

1. **Life Path Number**
   Because our life path number highlights the issues and challenges we have set for our self in this lifetime, when we take the time to

review the life path number of the other person in the relationship, we can begin to understand more about the issues and challenges **they** have chosen to face in this lifetime. This can then help us to understand how we could help them on their path, rather than hinder them by embarking upon a path of conflict.

2. **Destiny Number**
    Because our destiny number highlights the context within which we play out our life, then when we compare this number with that of another person, we can begin to understand why certain perspectives are important to them, and why they feel compelled to act in certain ways.

Because the universe is underpinned by continuums we often find that relationships are built upon opposites – we tend to experience that which we believe we are, through that which we believe we are not. It is this dynamic tension between these two positions that fuel the emotions and characteristics of all relationships to a greater or lesser extent. It is common to have relationships based upon one of four alternative perspectives.

In "**Positive-Peak**" relationships, the other person in the relationship tends to demonstrate skills or attributes that we do not have (but are learning about in this incarnation), and this can act as a catalyst for our own growth as we strive to emulate them.

In "**Negative-Peak**" relationships, the other person in the relationship tends to demonstrate skills or attributes that we do not have (but are learning about in this incarnation), but rather than act as a catalyst for our own growth, we tend to see these characters as a threat in some way, which often results in conflict as the result of jealousy or envy.

In "**Negative-Trough**" relationships, the other person in the relationship tends to act as a mirror for our own failings, and reflects back at us, through their own behaviour, characteristics or attributes which we dislike in our self. Often, as the result of our failure to see the gift in such relationships, they tend to result in dislike or conflict.

In "**Positive-Trough**" relationships, the other person in the relationship tends to act as a mirror for our own failings, and reflects back at us, through their own behaviour, characteristics or attributes that we dislike in our self. But rather than allow these relationships to deteriorate into dislike or conflict, we respond in a positive way, and attempt to see the gift, thereby (in time) transcending the relationship theme.

Because of the nature of certain relationships, (particularly with casual friends or colleagues), it is not always possible to accurately establish the information needed to be able to work out the other person's Destiny number (primarily because we may not know their full birth name). It is often much easier to obtain the information needed to calculate a person's life path number, (their date of birth) and in doing so, calculate our **Joint Path** number.

The way to work out a joint path with another person is as follows.

> Step 1 – Work out our own life path number, (as shown in the chapter 13)
>
> Step 2 – Work out the life path number of the other person (using the same method)
>
> Step 3 – Add both path numbers together, and reduce to number between 1 and 9

Note: other methods for calculating relationship paths involve the subtraction of life path numbers to establish the "Stress Number", but I have found that the addition of the numbers (rather than the subtraction) produces consistently better information.

The broad themes we can expect from joint path relationships are outlined in Table 5 below.

Number	Relationship Themes / Issues
1	Creativity, individuality, dependence, independence, assertiveness.
2	Compromise, co-operation, patience, contrast, balance.
3	Self expression, sensitivity, emotions, enthusiasm, joy.
4	Stability, process, endurance, hard work, practicality.
5	Freedom, discipline, travel, rebelliousness, sexuality.
6	Vision, acceptance, family, duty, perfectionism.
7	Study, knowledge, analysis, solitude, intuition.
8	Power, abundance, control, recognition, achievement.
9	Wisdom, integrity, spirituality, completion, the universe.
11	Creative Service, Illumination for Humanity, Inspiration
22	Creative Service, Building for Humanity
33	Creative Service, Healing Love

Table 5: Joint Life Path Themes

It is common for an individual to have a number of relationships that all have the same joint life path number (i.e. all share the same theme), but that feel very different to each other. This is because each relationship will vary in intensity depending upon the energy profile of the individuals involved, as well as whether the theme of the joint path is being played out in a positive or a negative way.

Chapter 16: Harmonics

A critical point to grasp if we are to arrive at a deeper understanding of our day-to-day life is the role of harmonics.

As mentioned previously, we choose our specific date and time of birth because this establishes the cosmic alignment necessary to create the energy profile which underpins our life plan to establish an energy pattern which repeats in nine year cycles. This cosmic alignment links the experiential themes chosen for our life plan with a timeline through which circumstances, events and experiences can be brought to us at a planned time, but can also be re-presented to us (again and again if necessary) if we miss a decision point.

By understanding this, we can begin to understand more about the energy profiles which are currently prevalent in our life, and hence begin to understand why particular events are occurring at a particular time, and as our level of consciousness grows, we can even begin to anticipate these experiences.

The key harmonics are Personal Year, Personal Month and Personal Day and to a lesser extent, our physical, emotional and intellectual biorhythms.

Personal Year

The calculation for your personal year for someone with a date of birth of 24/08/1962 is as follows:

1. Write out your date of birth in a DD/MM/YYYY format - 24/08/1963.
2. Substitute the year portion (YYYY) with the current year. So if the current year is 2005, then the new date would read 24/08/2005

3. Reduce this date down to a single number between 1 and 9 (as shown in chapter 13).

$$24 + 08 + 2005$$
$$6 + 8 + 2 + 5$$
$$14 + 7$$
$$21$$
$$\mathbf{3}$$

In this example, therefore, the key theme for this calendar year will relate to "Expression & Sensitivity", which means that during this year, the person with this harmonic profile will continually draw to them experiences, events or circumstances which relate to the theme of "expression" giving them the opportunity to express themselves more positively or to avoid negative expression, or perhaps, even to start expressing their feelings. On the "sensitivity" side, the events, circumstances and experiences are likely to relate to not only what we say (or don't say, depending upon whether we are working with the positive or negative side of this theme), but also "the way we say it" (or the way it is said to us or about us). The key personal year themes are outlined in table 6.

Year	Themes / Issue
1	Creativity, individuality, dependence, independence, assertiveness.
2	Compromise, co-operation, patience, contrast, balance.
3	Self expression, sensitivity, emotions, enthusiasm, joy.
4	Stability, process, endurance, hard work, practicality.
5	Freedom, discipline, travel, rebelliousness, sexuality.
6	Vision, acceptance, family, duty, perfectionism.
7	Study, knowledge, analysis, solitude, intuition.
8	Power, abundance, control, recognition, achievement.
9	Wisdom, integrity, spirituality, completion, the universe.

Table 6: Personal Year Themes

Personal Month

To calculate our personal month, we add the number calculated for our personal year (in the above example this was 3), to the number of the month and reduce these to a number between 1 and 9.

For example, if our personal year number is 3 and the current month is May (the 5th month), the personal month number is calculated as follows:

Month number (May) + Personal Year Number
5   +   3
8

In this example, the personal year number of 3 is added to the month number 5 (where January=1, February=2, March=3, April=4, May=5, June=6, July=7, August=8, September=9, October=10=1, November=11=2 and December=12=3) to give a personal month number of 8 which relates to the theme of "Power & Abundance".

During a personal month underpinned by "Power & Abundance" energy we may draw to us a series of experiences, events or circumstances relating to being powerful or powerless (depending upon whether we are working with the positive side or the negative side of the energy), authority, control and/or abundance. So during this month, we may draw to our self perhaps conflict with an authority figure – such as our boss – which uses the themes of power, authority and control; or perhaps get involved in a dispute with the bank, which uses the themes of power, control, authority and financial abundance.

Personal Day

To calculate our personal day we add the personal month number to the number of the day and reduce to a single figure between 1 and 9.

For example, if today is the 15th day of the month, this would be calculated as follows:

Day number (15th) + Personal Month Number
15   +   8
23
5

On a day with a theme of 5 the experiences, events and circumstances we will draw to our self are likely to relate to the theme of "Freedom & Discipline". This means that on this particular day, we will draw to our self events which allow us to explore the themes of "freedom" – such as an opportunity to book a holiday; or "discipline" – such as getting to the gym.

Because the energy associated with the personal year lasts much longer (i.e. the whole year), it is consequently a much stronger influence and takes precedence over the more subtle energies associated with the personal month or the personal day. Similarly, because the energy associated with the personal month is stronger than those associated with the personal day, then this will take precedence over the personal day energy.

It is as a result of our overarching harmonic profile that we derive our physical biorhythm pattern (which underpins our strength, health and physical vitality and has a wave cycle of 23 days), our emotional biorhythm pattern (which underpins our emotional stability and has a wave cycle of 28 days) and our intellectual biorhythm (which underpins our verbal, mathematical, symbolic, creative reasoning capacities and has a wave cycle of 33 days).

This detailed interplay of energies and themes is used as part of the process of designing our life path. When energies align – where we have the same energy number underpinning our personal year, personal month and personal day, then this can facilitate much more intense experiences or events. So watch out!

As we try to facilitate a deeper understanding of our day-to-day situations, events and circumstances it is important that we continually ask our self what is the theme or themes which are playing out here? It is also critical that we also ask our self why is this happening now, at this time, in this place and with these people?

By understanding the harmonics of our personal year, personal month and personal day (and to a lesser extent our physical, emotional and intellectual biorhythms), we are better positioned to understand the context of the events which happen in our life.

Initially, the time taken between an event happening and our awareness to ask the "what? and why? questions" can be days, months or even years. But with continual awareness and practice, we eventually develop a level of awareness which allows us to ask these questions as events are in the process of unfolding. Once we get to this level of awareness, this gives us a good chance of avoiding being sucked into the negative dynamics which can result from events and add to the turbulence of our life.

By understanding more about how the harmonics of life facilitate our day-to-day, month-to-month and year-to-year experiences, we can better understand the ebb and flow of events, circumstances and experiences throughout our life and the lives of others with whom our world collides. It is the collision of our individual worlds – each of which is underpinned by different harmonic profiles – which creates the world we see around us.

The way that these harmonics play themselves out within an organisation (organisational harmonics) is covered in more detail in my next book.

Chapter 17: The Wheel of Consciousness

I developed "The Wheel of Consciousness" as a tool with which to measure my perceived level of consciousness, and by which I could monitor any progress I believe I was making along a spiritual path. When I thought about the topic of "Consciousness" I felt that there were four themes which underpinned the notion of consciousness: body, mind, soul and spirit. In designing the Wheel of Consciousness, therefore, I represented these themes by segmenting the wheel into four quadrants.

The Wheel of Consciousness is outlined in diagram 21, with descriptions relating to each segment outlined in the tables below. (Blank copies of this diagram can be downloaded from my website www.resonanceprinciple. com).

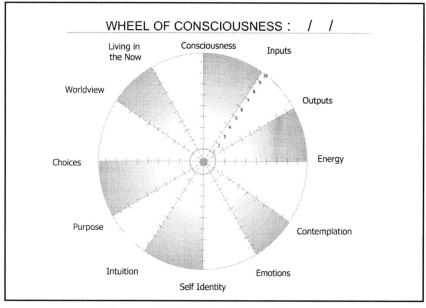

Diagram 21 – The Wheel of Consciousness

Each segment of the wheel is marked from 1 to 10, with a score of 1 being represented by the check mark at the point closest to the centre, and a score of 10 being represented by the circumference of the wheel. So, if when considering the category labelled "Inputs" I assess my own score as "4", then I would simply move to the fourth check mark up from the centre on the axis labelled **"Inputs"** and put an "X" in that position.

Before you begin to assess your own response to each segment of the wheel, however, I would recommend that you read the descriptions relating to each segment and take a moment to consider your score before completing.

The first quadrant deals with our level of awareness on the theme of **"Body"**.

SEGMENT	BODY
1. Inputs	How aware are you of the impact of the substances you put into your body? At level 10, you actively choose healthy foods and avoid substances that lower your energy levels such as coffee, sugar, nicotine and alcohol – i.e. your body is a temple. At level 1 you do not give any thought to what you put into you body, i.e. your body is a dustbin.
2. Outputs	How aware are you of your outputs, e.g. your language and behaviours? At level 10, you are conscious of your connection to others and reflect this in your language and behaviour – you recognise that all aspects of your behaviour causes ripples either positive or negative and act accordingly. At level 1, you pay little regard to your language or behaviour, and give little or no consideration to how your language and behaviour impacts upon others.
3. Energy	How do you get your energy? At a level 10, you are conscious of your existence as an energy being in an energy universe, and therefore make a conscious attempt generate your own energy from inspiration. At level 1, you are unconscious of your energy state, and therefore attempt to get your energy by stealing it from others, generally through manipulation.

The second quadrant deals with our level of awareness on the theme of
"Mind".

SEGMENT	MIND
4. Contemplation	How aware are you of your level of contemplation? At a level 10, you have a strict programme of contemplation and / or meditation. At a level 1, you rarely, if ever, spend time contemplating and never meditating.
5. Emotions	How in touch with your emotions are you? At a level 10, you freely acknowledge and express your emotions in all circumstances. At level 1, you routinely repress or block the true expression of your emotions which then manifest in another way such as anger or aggression.
6. Self Identity	How do you define yourself? At a level 10, you define who you are in holistic terms. At level 1, you define yourself by the job you do or the things you have.

The third quadrant deals with our level of awareness on the theme of
"soul".

SEGMENT	SOUL
7. Intuition	How aware are you of your intuition? At a level 10, you listen to your intuition and follow it every time. At a level 1, you sometimes hear it, but ignore it – or you do not recognise when and how it speaks to you.
8. Purpose	How aware are you of your "Purpose"? At a level 10, you know what you are here to do, and consistently make decisions that move you towards this purpose. At level 1, you do not give any thought to purpose and continue with life on a day-to-day basis.
9. Choices	How aware are you of the choices you make on a moment-to-moment basis? At a level 10, you are continually aware that you are making choices every moment and that the choices you are making are intended to move you towards your perceived purpose. At a level 1, you simply muddle through, with no conscious direction.

The fourth quadrant deals with our level of awareness on the theme of **"spirit"**.

SEGMENT	SPIRIT
10. Worldview	How do you view the world? At a level 10, you view the world as a living entity, which you share with all other life forms and with which we interact on a day-to-day basis through our choices. At a level 1, you view the world as a resource for your personal consumption.
11. Living in the Now	How aware are you of the present moment? At level 10 you consciously live your life with an awareness and appreciation for each moment. At a level 1, you consistently plan for the future and reflect on the past or opt out completely by using substances to get you through the day.
12. Consciousness	In this final sector, you need to reflect on the previous 11 sectors in order to gauge your overall level of consciousness. This sector should really reflect the average of the others. If you have a low level of awareness in the previous sectors, then this sector should reflect this. If, however, you have a consistently high level of awareness in the previous sectors, then this sector will reflect that high level of overall consciousness.

Once you have scored each segment with an "X" at what you consider to be a reflective score, then you can simply join up the "X's" to form a shape, (see the example in diagram 22).

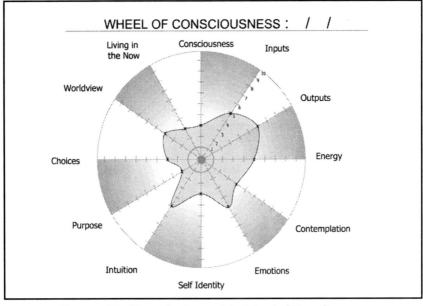

Diagram 22 – Example of complete Wheel of Consciousness

116

Imagine that the highest level of consciousness and spiritual awareness is represented by a perfect circle shape, with each segment achieving the maximum value of 10. Now compare this perfect and full circle shape to the shape of your own Wheel of Consciousness – how do they compare?

The most common mistake I come across when people complete the Wheel of Consciousness is that we tend to score ourselves too highly. This happens, not because we are being dishonest, but rather, because **"we don't know what we don't know"**. In other words, most people are unaware of their level of ignorance. Because we may have read a few books on a specific topic, we can sometimes believe that we have covered it all, when in fact, there is much more material of which we are unaware at this point in our journey. So, if (according to you) you have scored 8s, 9s or 10s on your Wheel of Consciousness, then congratulations – because this puts you right up there with the great spiritual leaders and gurus. For most people reading this book, I would expect a more realistic level is likely to be in the 4s or 5s.

I would recommend that you complete a new Wheel of Consciousness every few months. Each time you complete a new Wheel of Consciousness, then compare the new wheel with your previously completed wheels, in order to try to gauge any sense of progress. As you complete each new wheel, do it without reference to the previous wheel so that you are not influenced by the previous scores.

As with any self improvement activity, awareness is only part of the solution. If we want to develop our level of consciousness, then we need to take some positive action towards improvement. I have outlined the development aid that I use in diagram 23.

DEVELOPMENT NEEDS

List below some of the areas which you may
need to develop further in order to develop your
level of consciousness.

1. _____

2. _____

3. _____

4. _____

EXAMPLE: 1. Introduce a healthy eating regime
               2. Exercise 3 times per week for 30 mins
               3. Meditate for 15 mins each day

Diagram 23: Development Plan

Each month, when I complete a new Wheel of Consciousness, I set myself tasks to complete in the coming month, with the aim of trying to improve my overall level of consciousness. The discipline of doing this acts as a mechanism to keep my journey towards consciousness in the forefront of my mind. Without this tool it is easy to be overwhelmed by the level of noise in our daily life, and therefore lose our way. I would recommend that you set a target of no more than one improvement action for each quadrant (Body, Mind, Soul & Spirit) per month, else the likelihood is that you will be overwhelmed. Try to make progress in each quadrant each month, and review regularly.

Chapter 18: A Family Plan

As I mentioned in the introduction, this book is being written primarily as a life guide for my daughter Emma (who at the time of writing is 7 years old), in the hope that I can pass on some information to her which may be of use as she tries to make her way in the world.

In this section, therefore, I have used some of the tools outlined in the previous chapters as a mechanism for her to gain some more detailed insights into her own family, and in doing so, I hope that it not only demonstrates the practical use of the tools, but that it will also provide Emma with a unique perspective of her parents and her family environment.

Vibrational Profile Chart: Phil Holmes

The vibrational energy profile for myself is outlined in diagram 24.

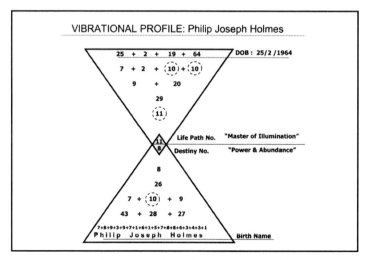

Diagram 24: Vibrational Profile – Philip Joseph Holmes

Life Path Number: 29 /11

My life path number is a "Master" number, so therefore much is expected during this lifetime. The path of an 11 is that of a "Master of Illumination". This indicates that my life issues will be concerned with inspiration and illumination. Because of the increased vibration of this path, it can mean that if approached in a negative way, it can result in the same attributes as those of the negative life path number 2 (11 reduced down to 2), and can lead to me being indecisive, moody and withdrawn.

The energy associated with this life path has the attributes of charisma and leadership, so if I can master the lessons in the earlier stages of this path, the next phase could include becoming an inspirational leader (which links with my Destiny number). The mission on this path is to be someone others look to for truth, wisdom and illumination. The number 9 energy as part of the composite of the 11, means that integrity is a key part of my path, therefore, whatever I choose to do has to be true to universal principles and aligned to a higher purpose.

Because, ultimately, this path relates to illumination, inspiration and creative service, then the careers that I will succeed most in are likely to be careers which put me in the spotlight, or in which I work with groups or inspire others in some way.

The lessons for me on this path, however, relate to confidence. Before I can unlock all of my creative potential to illuminate or inspire others, I must firstly overcome my own fears and insecurities, which are amplified due the double impact of number 1 energy that makes the 11 path. As a result, my childhood was spent facing issues relating to confidence, and through my teenage years and early adult life the issues in my life related to increasing my level of confidence in my own abilities and gradually reducing my reliance on the opinion of others. Now, as an adult, when I am operating on the positive side of my energy profile, I can be seen as charismatic and inspirational. When operating on the negative side on my energy profile, however, I can be seen as inhibited, aloof and insecure. During bouts of negativity, because my creative energy is blocked, this can result in the physical manifestation of lower back pain.

Destiny Number: 8

With a destiny number of 8, my purpose is to use my skills in the context of business and organisations. The destiny number 8 can often invoke the qualities of being visionary and also the qualities of leadership, which is why this number often relates to material success. It can also mean that I have challenges associated with recognition, authority and money along the way.

Birth Names:

My birth name profile can be defined as follows:

The first name of "**Philip**" has a value of 7, which means that I have chosen to have a strong mind, which helps me to research, analyse facts and draw conclusions, whilst being both perceptive and good at dealing with people. The flip side, however, can be that I will often be thoughtful, solitary and at times even secretive. It can also mean that I have a degree of impatience which could keep me from seeing things through to completion.

The middle name of "**Joseph**" has a value of 10, reduced to 1, which re-enforces the creativity, confidence and leadership elements on my path.

The surname of "**Holmes**" has a value of 9 and enforces the pursuit of wisdom and the need to use this wisdom with integrity. When growing up in the Holmes family, I was often taught about "rightness", "fairness" and "integrity".

When I consider all these numbers together I can create the following short synopsis about the life I have chosen this time around:

- The life path along which I will travel this life-time is dominated by the theme of Creativity & Confidence.
- Before I can fully unlock my creative potential, I must transcend all of the issues presented to me relating to my own confidence levels.

- A key part of my childhood conditioning occurred precisely to set up confidence barriers, which I could learn to overcome as part of my life path.
- Because this path is a Master number path, the vibration levels are higher and this will have the effect of making the lessons harder, but the rewards (in terms of growth) greater.
- When I consider that the themes of my life path relate to illumination and creative service (master No. 11) by transcending creativity and confidence issues, then I have chosen to summarise this path in the following way: "**overcome your confidence issues to create something which will illuminate a path for others**".
- The destiny number of 8 means that it is the application of my skills in the world of business which resonates very strongly with me. In terms of illuminating a path, therefore, the path which resonates most strongly with me is the path of authenticity in business, i.e. attempting to integrate the spiritual themes of "rightness", "fairness", "connectedness", "sustainability" and "authenticity" with those of business, i.e. profitability and shareholder wealth.
- The more I give license to my creativity, the better I feel. The more I ignore my creativity, however, the more I can feel moody, withdrawn and indecisive, and often this blocking of creativity results in the physical manifestation of lower back pain, which occurs as the result of a blocked energy centre (charka) at the base of the spine. In order to keep my creative centres open, I need to exercise regularly.
- The sense of vision that comes from this path means that I can often see solutions that no one else can see. The downside, however, is that because these solutions tend to be ahead of their time, they are often not fully recognised by others. If I am not vigilant then lessons resulting from such situations can impact upon my level of confidence, thereby creating a vicious circle.
- A characteristic of this path is that it feels rather like being a pioneer, in that, I am trying to work with solutions that few, if any, other people have considered. This can lead to feelings of isolation, and again, can set up a vicious circle relating to confidence.

- With a first name number of 7, this energy supports the capacity for research and investigation required for illumination. This number also creates a dynamic tension because associated with this number is a desire for privacy, but associated with the master number life path, are skills which could put me in the spotlight.

Vibrational Profile Chart: Maureen Holmes

The vibrational profile for Mary Maureen Holmes – my wife and Emma's mother - is outlined in diagram 25.

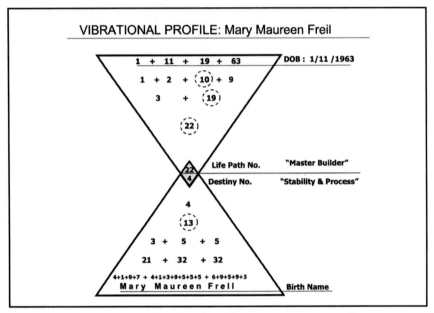

Diagram 25: Vibrational Profile – Mary Maureen Freil

Life Path Number: 22/4

This life path number is also a "Master" number, so again, much is expected of anyone on this path. The path of a 22 is that of a "Master Builder", which means that on this path Maureen needs to express her highest vibration through organisation and planning, in order to build something of lasting value for humanity. This path exists to convert dreams into a reality (note that the birth date numbers have not been reduced further because by cross checking using the "adding across" method and the "adding down" both highlight a master number path of 22).

This path demands self-mastery. The challenges associated with this path are not only those of a 4, but also those of a 2, which are doubled through the expression as 22. As part of this path, Maureen will have to work hard to overcome challenges relating to discipline, practicality and organisation. The influence of the 22 means that Maureen will feel drawn to big projects and will like to set big goals, but key challenges arise from her ability to co-operate with others long enough to see the completion of these projects. The challenges of a 4 mean that Maureen can become overwhelmed with the tasks she set herself and seeks to move on to new projects, leaving previous projects incomplete. A critical element to this path relates to challenges with building and maintaining a "process".

The life path of a 4 can include a difficult family history, with strong characters setting up negative conditioning in relation to foundations and stability. Ultimately, however, as with all master number paths, this path relates to being of service to mankind. In order to be of best service to mankind, Maureen needs to learn that success can only be achieved through co-operation with others and by using her organisational skills and practical know-how to build something of lasting worth. By choosing to be born of the 1st day of the month, Maureen has chosen to have a strong, independent spirit and a desire to lead. The energy of a 1 also means that Maureen can be innovative, courageous, highly individual, forceful with her ideas and good at giving orders (but not necessarily good at taking orders).

Destiny Number: 4
With a Destiny number of 4, Maureen's purpose is to build. A Destiny number of 4 relates to managing, organising and working hard to ensure that whatever she builds is of lasting value.

Name Numbers:
Maureen's birth name profile can be defined as follows: the first name of "**Mary**" has a value of 3 which enforces her need for social interaction, communication and expression. The 3 energy underpins the need for Maureen to learn to empathise with others without overwhelming them. There is also an underlying sensitivity to criticism as well as a temptation towards the extravagant, the frivolous and the superficial.

The middle name of "**Maureen**" and the surname of "**Freil**" both have a value of 5 which enforces the struggle to find a balance between the need for freedom and independence and the inner requirements of discipline and commitment.

When considering all these numbers together, the following short synopsis can be created:

- The life path along which Maureen will travel in this lifetime is dominated by the theme of Stability & Process.
- Maureen's life path of 22 is that of a Master Builder. She is here to create something of lasting value for humanity.
- Before Maureen can fully unlock her true potential, however, she needs to overcome issues relating to "Stability & Process". It is only by learning how to establish and consistently adhere to the processes she develops, that she will be able to achieve a degree of stability, through which her full potential can be reached.
- Another critical theme for Maureen is that encapsulated by the number 2 - "Co-operation & Balance". Because Maureen's life path number is 22, this means that the impact of the number 2 energy is doubled. Maureen is likely, therefore, to face some intense issues relating to "Co-operation" i.e. how to get on with people, which is likely to be characterised by high degrees of co-operation (getting along with everyone), followed by low degrees of co-operation (not getting along with anyone).
- The constant see-sawing that underpins the theme of co-operation is likely to produce mini dramas on a day-to-day or week-to-week basis, until Maureen can learn to achieve more of a balance.
- The karmic number of 13 highlighted in her birth name chart indicates that Maureen is carrying karmic issues from previous lives relating to "Work", in which she may not have taken her full share of the load, and as such, it is likely that extra responsibility will be expected during this lifetime.
- The karmic number of 19 highlighted in her Pythagorean triangle, indicates that Maureen is also carrying karmic issues relating to "Power" into this lifetime. It is likely that in previous lives, therefore, Maureen has in some way abused the power she had, and as a

result, will draw issues to herself on the themes of independence, consideration and assertion, which provide an opportunity to learn how to use power in an appropriate way, and how to stand up for herself.

- A key part of Maureen's childhood conditioning comes through two critical numbers. The surname number of 5 (relating to her maiden name of Freil), indicates that within this family there would have been issues relating to "Freedom & Discipline". The other critical number is Maureen's reduced life path number of 4 (i.e. 22 reduced to 4), which tends to set up family conditioning involving a lack of stability.

Vibrational Profile Chart: Emma Holmes

The vibrational profile for Emma Catherine Holmes is outlined in diagram 26.

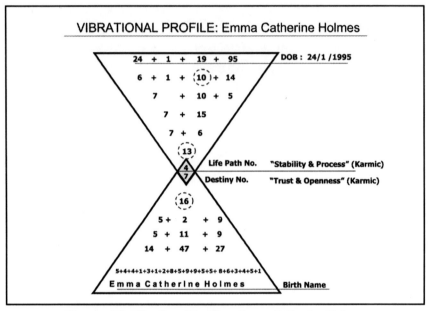

Diagram 26: Vibrational Profile – Emma Catherine Holmes

Life Path Number: 13/4

With a karmic life path of 13/4 Emma is working through issues relating to stability, creativity, emotional expression and learning to build a step-by-step process. Emma will need to overcome self doubt and insecurity in order to develop her level of personal confidence. The value of the 3 as a component part of her life path means that she will have to learn to express herself, and the value of the 1 means that she will have a strong creative drive. Early childhood experiences will generally relate to establishing a strong foundation. With this path, there can be a tendency to set big goals, but the life lessons relate to how she needs to develop a step-by-step approach to processes in order to break large goals down into more manageable chunks. Because this won't come easy, Emma will, at times, feel frustrated with process issues. This path couples the inherent impatience of a 4, with the creative inspiration of a 1 to set up a path underpinned by unrealistic expectations, and a desire for success without going through the process to get there. By choosing to be born on the 24th, both the 2 energy, and the 4 energy mean that she will be both hardworking and fair. When these numbers are reduced to the energy of a 6, it also indicates that she will like things to do with home and family.

Destiny Number: 16 / 7

With a Destiny number of 7, Emma's purpose relates to research and analysis. Her purpose is to use her skill at research and her drive for perfectionism to seek out wisdom. This path can often be linked with education in all its forms.

With a karmic destiny number (16/7), however, Emma is likely to have many intense issues relating to the theme of love. In the past it is likely that Emma has abused love in some form, either as a result of a lack of integrity with the feelings of others, or as a result of family or commitment which caused suffering to others.

Name Numbers:

Emma's birth name profile can be defined as follows: the first name of "**Emma**" has a value of 5 which enforces the struggle to find balance between the need for freedom and independence and the inner requirements for discipline and commitment.

The middle name of "**Catherine**" has a value of 2 which enforces the need to co-operate with others in order to progress through life.

The surname of "**Holmes**" has a value 9 which enforces the pursuit of wisdom and the need to use this wisdom with integrity.

When considering all these numbers together, the following synopsis can be created:

- Emma is here to work through issues relating to stability, creativity and emotional expression.

- She needs to balance creativity, strength and sensitivity in a positive way in order to make her life path easier. If she can't then they could end up working against each other and result in frustration.
- The learning about process is the key to success on this life path. The more she sticks to the processes she develops the easier her life will be. It's not so much about the destination as the journey (process).
- Because she will have to overcome self-doubt and insecurity, she needs to develop her levels of personal confidence and often confront tendencies towards lack of commitment and instability.
- The path of a 4 can lead to a desire for status, and she may develop a big ego in order to compensate for her insecurity.
- 4s benefit from a stable home life and childhood issues can relate to establishing a stable foundation.
- 4s need to express their emotions and often these lessons are presented either by their own children or by other children (see next section on Christopher Holmes).
- The impatience of a 4 linked with the creative inspiration of a 1 means that she will often want things to happen quickly if not instantaneously.
- As parents, we have tried to teach her about how to develop a "Step-by-step" approach to the processes in her life, because we believe that by doing so we are giving her the best possible chance to achieve stability, success and happiness in her life. This is why we have been more forceful about "completing the last few steps" i.e. the full life-cycle of the process, rather than the first few steps or completing only 80% of the process.
- This is also why we have encouraged her to get involved with activities that focus on step-by-step. For Emma, this has been easier to achieve through physical activities, such as ice-skating or football. Our belief is that by helping Emma realise that the more she sticks to and repeats the process (i.e. practises) the more she improves, thereby achieving her desired goal (to be a good ice-skater or to be good at football).
- Our focus, therefore, was on teaching her how to break tasks or

goals down into smaller chunks, in order to try to give her a better chance of achieving the end point, as well as (more importantly) allowing her to see that this is how she can achieve success in her own life.

- Because my wife's life path also strongly relates to the issues of process, this is why it often fell to me to try to ensure consistency and reinforce the need for process.
- Our goal as parents, therefore, has been to try to provide a stable home environment which would allow Emma to feel secure. To encourage her at every opportunity in order to minimise any issues relating to self-doubt. To encourage her to be more patient and to help her to develop a step-by-step approach to any problem, issue or goal, and to encourage her to see tasks through to completion.

Vibrational Profile Chart: Christopher Holmes

The vibration profile for Christopher Freil Holmes is outlined in diagram 27.

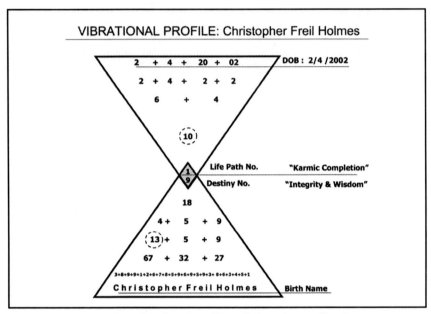

VIBRATIONAL PROFILE: Christopher Freil Holmes

DOB : 2/4 /2002

2 + 4 + 20 + 02
2 + 4 + 2 + 2
6 + 4

(10)

Life Path No.   "Karmic Completion"
Destiny No.   "Integrity & Wisdom"

18
4 + 5 + 9
(13) + 5 + 9
67 + 32 + 27
3+8+9+9+1+2+6+7+8+5+9+6+9+5+9+3+ 8+6+3+4+5+1
Christopher Freil Holmes   Birth Name

Diagram 27: Vibrational Profile – Christopher Freil Holmes

This path is unusual, in that Christopher was born with a genetic disorder known as "Trisomy 18" also known as "Edward's Syndrome", where the life expectancy is greatly reduced. Consequently, children born with this disorder are not expected to live for more than 12 months.

Christopher died, aged six months old.

Life Path Number: 10 / 1
The life path of 10 is a karmic life path relating to "Completion".

By choosing to be born on the 2nd day of the month, this indicates that a key part of his life plan was to provide balance and harmony, as well as to impart the universal energy related to mediation and peacemaking.

Destiny Number: 9
With a destiny number 9, Christopher's mission in this life was to perfect and love unconditionally.

Name Numbers:
Christopher's birth name profile can be defined as follows: the first name of "**Christopher**" has a value of 4 which enforces need to establish a process in order to attain a degree of stability. In Christopher's case this happened much more on a physical level, rather than a mental or emotional level.

The middle name of "**Freil**" has a value of 5 and enforces the need to find balance between the need for freedom and independence and the inner requirements of discipline and commitment. The surname of "**Holmes**" has a value of 9 and enforces the use of wisdom in line with integrity.

Chapter 19: Conclusions

So what have I learned on my journey so far?

There is an old proverb that states "it is a wise man who knows that he doesn't know", and the further I journey towards spirit, the more apt this saying seems to be. The paradox seems to be that the further I journey towards "spirit", the more complex the universe seems to be, and consequently, the less I seem to know. It has often been said that man cannot know the mind of God, and I think this is true.

If this dimension is an illusion, then the likelihood is that we cannot – at this stage of our evolution - know how the illusion works. The best we can hope for, is to accept the wonder of the illusion, and, as best we can, play our part in that illusion.

Throughout my journey, I have tried to simplify the complex ideas, which holistically make up the process of spirituality. I have consolidated these many ideas into what I believe are the 5 tenets of spirituality. These tenets, which have been consistent over my many years of searching, are:

1.   All is One
All matter is part of something larger. This means that each atom, molecule, plant, animal, and human is part of something larger. The label for this larger thing varies. Some call it God, Godhead, Source, or Universal Consciousness – but the belief that we are all fragments of this larger force is consistent. This notion is becoming integrated with mainstream science through the development of the "Big Bang" theory. Given that there was nothing in the universe before the Big Bang, and given that all matter in the universe was generated as a result of this singularity, and given that matter cannot be created or destroyed, then we are all here as a direct result of the same singularity, and consequently, we are all part

of the same thing.

2.   All is energy

From a spiritual perspective, our human form is the result of an underlying energy pattern. From a scientific perspective, it is now more widely accepted that objects which appear solid (rocks, trees, and even humans) are, at their lowest level, simply energy vibrating at differing rates. There is nothing in our universe that is not made up from energy. We are energy beings in an energy universe.

3.   All lives have a purpose

From some spiritual perspectives, this purpose is Enlightenment, or Nirvana or Tao. For others, however, the purpose is about learning either on an individual basis or as part of a collective learning. Either way, the notion of purpose, and a process of growth towards the realisation of this purpose, is a key underpinning of the process of spirituality.

4.   All paths are chosen

Each one of us has the power to choose between up or down, left or right, sickness or health, good or evil. Our choices are woven together to form our life plan, and we continue to choose every minute of every day, thereafter.

The true notion of free will operates at a much higher level, and consequently, the majority of our choices are made at a higher level than the physical realm; our range of choices on this plane is therefore, much narrower than we may think – but we are free to make plans!!

5.   All return to One

At the end of our life, we return back to where we came from. For some this is Heaven, for others, the spiritual realm, but either way, we return.

Our perspective on the human race seems to me to be warped. I believe that the human form is simply a vehicle for the development of consciousness – and not a very well developed one in the overall scheme of things. Yes, we are more developed than animals in most cases. Our species, however, lives in the 3rd dimension, and there are many, many levels of development above where even the most evolved human is now. Our assumption that we are the most evolved creature in the universe is therefore, I believe, arrogance of the highest order.

I do not believe that humanity has a particularly special place in the order of the universe. From a universal perspective, we are a lower form of life, but we are still evolving. As with all evolving systems, humanity must either learn to evolve or it too will become extinct – we have no special dispensation.

The bottom line is that whilst there are many people around us to support us as we journey through this lifetime, at the end of the day, **we make this journey alone**. We have all the time we are ever going to get – it's just a question of how we decide to use that time. The race is long, but it is only with our self. Life is a game. It is not the winning or losing that counts, but how we play the game. Sometimes to win is to lose. What good if a man profit by the whole world, but lose his soul?

Remember, nothing happens by chance. Every person, and all the events in your life are there because you have drawn them there – what you choose to do with them is up to you.

Good luck.

<u>**Appendix 1 – Life Path Summary**</u>

LIFE PATH : 1 – CREATIVITY & CONFIDENCE

Your Life Path number identifies the challenges which you will face and the specific issues to be confronted on your journey through life. Remember that it will be necessary to overcome the negative expressions of your number energy to realise your highest potential.

The main theme in a life path #1 is the need to harness and direct your dynamic, amplified energy to find a creative & responsible outlet for self expression.

Life Challenges:

As a 1 you act and feel different. You have a unique vision and worldview, but often this is the source of problems. Many 1's may suffer feelings of uncertainty, insecurity, inadequacy, inequality and the need for approval arising out of a subconscious sense of "aloneness". These fears must be faced and overcome. 1's abundant energy requires innovative and bold expression, therefore you must develop confidence, self assurance and discipline to channel your strong determination to constructive ends.

Positive Characteristics:	*Negative Characteristics:*
Independent / pioneering	→ Self centred / arrogant
Strong willed / focused	→ Stubborn / domineering
Ambitious / courageous	→ Impulsive / aggressive
Innovative / spontaneous	→ Impatient / seeks instant gratification
Vital / enthusiastic	→ Pushy / opinionated

The extent to which you embrace your life path will determine whether you are expressing and experiencing the negative or the positive aspects of your specific life energy.

Negative Expression:

When life challenges are not faced or successfully resolved, your energy may be blocked, positive expression is repressed and the following problems may be experienced:

- Insecurity / emotional neediness
- Obsessive independence
- Over dependency / inability to support yourself
- Addictive behaviour e.g. over eating / substance abuse.

Remedies:

- For insecurity – constructive visualisation / positive affirmation.
- For energy imbalance -alternative therapies e.g. acupuncture, acupressure, reiki, body work, vitamin supplements.
- Avoid over eating protein and fat.
- Get closer to nature.
- Exercise is more essential than for other life path numbers.
- Broaden focus from self to others by cultivating true friendship and awareness of human interests.

140

LIFE PATH : 2 – CO-OPERATION & BALANCE

Your Life Path number identifies the challenges which you will face and the specific issues to be confronted on your journey through life. Remember that it will be necessary to overcome the negative expressions of your number energy to realise your highest potential.

The main theme in a life path #2 is the need to overcome an exaggerated sense of your responsibility for others in order to achieve a balance with your inner needs and limits.

Life Challenges:
As a 2 you have an innate drive to serve and assist others however your desire to co-operate can be the source of problems. You must face and resolve your inner discord and conflict between the duality of opposite ideas: beliefs and values, self and others, giving and receiving, thoughts and feelings. It is important to avoid becoming a victim of your own willingness to help and support others as you may attract into your life those who will "use" you. Through such lessons you must begin to honour your own feelings and needs, and learn self-assertiveness to balance a tendency towards passive "martyrdom". 2's must overcome acute sensitivity and a tendency to over analysis and worry.

Positive Characteristics:
Gentle / sensitive
Supportive / helpful
Considerate / adaptable
Quiet / cautious
Persuasive / unselfish

Negative Characteristics:
→ **Timid / over emotional**
→ **Weak / indecisive**
→ **Dependant / needy**
→ **Withdrawn / moody**
→ **underhand / sneaky**

The extent to which you embrace your life path will determine whether you are expressing and experiencing the negative or the positive aspects of your specific life energy.

Negative Expression: When life challenges are not faced or successfully resolved, your energy may be blocked, positive expression is repressed and the following problems may be experienced:

- Physical / emotional / mental abuse
- Vulnerability / helplessness
- Emotional shutdown
- Stress / muscular tension

- Stubborn resistance / chronic resentment
- Anxiety / feeling overwhelmed
- Impotence / frigidity
- Allergies / immune and lymphatic system problems

Remedies:
- For flexibility and relaxation – yoga / meditation
- For subordinate tendency – self assertiveness, self expression training

LIFE PATH : 3 – EXPRESSION & SENSITIVITY

Your Life Path number identifies the challenges which you will face and the specific issues to be confronted on your journey through life. Remember that it will be necessary to overcome the negative expressions of your number energy to realise your highest potential.

The main theme in a life path #3 is the need to overcome self-doubt and fear of expression in order to develop your confidence and experience abundance.

Life Challenges:

As a 3 you have a powerful drive towards social interaction and communication, but this will require you to overcome your need to be liked and an underlying sensitivity to criticism, as well as the temptation towards the extravagant, frivolous and superficial. The challenge will be to acknowledge and express your authentic emotional self with an enthusiasm which inspires others to emotional openness and joy. 3's must learn to empathise with the troubles of others without getting overwhelmed by them, and to avoid emotional manipulation.

Positive Characteristics:	**Negative Characteristics:**
Expressive / articulate	Gossipy / outspoken
Enthusiastic / inspirational	Scattered energy / frivolous
Joyful / optimistic	Extravagant / impractical
Popular / witty	Moody / critical
Playful / light hearted	Untidy / wasteful

The extent to which you embrace your life path will determine whether you are expressing and experiencing the negative or the positive aspects of your specific life energy.

Negative Expression: When life challenges are not faced or successfully resolved, your energy may be blocked, positive expression is repressed and the following problems may be experienced:

-Over shyness, tongue tied, speech impediments
- Sexual guilt / perceived inadequacy
- Vulnerable to absorb the negative emotions of others

- Manic depression / feeling overwhelmed
- Over critical / hyper sensitive to criticism
- Suffer from an over-sensitive stomach when stressed.

Remedies:
- Focus and prioritise effort and use of energy
- Focus expressive talent on higher ideas to share with others
- Cultivate structure, purpose and commitment in life by using creative visualisation
- Avoid trivial social veneer, intolerance and gossip.

142

LIFE PATH : 4 – STABILITY & PROCESS

Your Life Path number identifies the challenges which you will face and the specific issues to be confronted on your journey through life. Remember that it will be necessary to overcome the negative expressions of your number energy to realise your highest potential.

The main theme in a life path #4 is the need to commit to patient & gradual progress towards clear goals and stability in your life.

Life Challenges:

As a 4 you must overcome impatience and ill founded ambition, and instead, focus effort on proper, step-by-step, preparation to establish practical skills and achieve security. The appeal of easy, magical solutions should be avoided in favour of commitment to inner stability. You must learn that achievement flows from clear intent and perseverance through difficulties. 4's may lose momentum when stuck on over analysis or minor details and may become discouraged working within the restrictions of a limited field. However, discipline and will power are required to overcome limitations.

Positive Characteristics:	Negative Characteristics:
Hard working / efficient	**Slow / over exact**
Serious / honest	**Boring / joyless**
Calm / down to earth	**Officious / unimaginative**
Responsible / tenacious	**Insecure / stubborn**
Respectable / trustworthy	**inflexible / suspicious**

The extent to which you embrace your life path will determine whether you are expressing and experiencing the negative or the positive aspects of your specific life energy.

Negative Expression: When life challenges are not faced or successfully resolved, your energy may be blocked, positive expression is repressed and the following problems may be experienced:

- Swing from confused & over analytical to impulsive
- Can become overwhelmed
- Irresponsibility / temporary effort without commitment

- Physically and psychologically rigid
- Obsessive over past mistakes and failures
- Frequent changes of job, home or relationship

A difficult family history is common with 4's as family represents foundation and stability issues which must be confronted and resolved.

Remedies:
- For physical rigidity - Yoga / Tai chi
- For psychological rigidity - Deep breathing / meditation
- For self-esteem issues find roles and jobs where talents and capabilities are valued
- Align yourself to others of higher vibrations and strive to expand your worldview

LIFE PATH : 5 – FREEDOM & DISCIPLINE

Your Life Path number identifies the challenges which you will face and the specific issues to be confronted on your journey through life. Remember that it will be necessary to overcome the negative expressions of your number energy to realise your highest potential.

The main theme in a life path #5 is the struggle to find a balance between your need for independence and freedom and the inner requirements of discipline and commitment.

Life Challenges:

The challenge for 5's is to transcend the tendency for sensual over-indulgence and learn that the truest freedom is based on the structure and stability that comes from self-discipline and self-mastery. As a 5 you may be prone to extreme independence including adventure and reckless risk-taking although many other 5's may choose the vicarious freedom and adventure of books and TV. Indecision and restlessness arising out of fear, doubt and negative thinking are central issues which you must face and overcome. 5's must learn that running away from routine and avoiding commitment is not the way to liberation. Your highest goal of inner freedom can only be attained by setting priorities and focusing your resourcefulness and inner strength to overcome the illusions of lack and limitation in life.

Positive Characteristics:

Enthusiastic / versatile

Adventurous / vivacious

Clever / quick thinking

Magnetic / free spirit

Adaptable / resourceful

Negative Characteristics:

Inconsistent / impulsive

Restless / risk taker

Inconsiderate / discontented

Unfaithful / sensually over indulgent

Impatient / unreliable

The extent to which you embrace your life path will determine whether you are expressing and experiencing the negative or the positive aspects of your specific life energy.

Negative Expression:
When life challenges are not faced or successfully resolved, your energy may be blocked, positive expression is repressed and the following problems may be experienced:

- Frustration
- Deep sense of inauthenticity
- Quick to judge and criticise
- Irresponsible / addictive behaviour
- Smothering parent or partner
- Manipulation of others to get your own way
- Quick temper / sharp tongue
- Promiscuous / lustful
- Exhaustion, adrenal stress and poor circulation
- Financial lack or even imprisonment

Remedies:
- A disciplined approach to diet
- Cultivate steadiness, discipline and focus on purpose
- Learn that all obstacles are for the highest good
- Use your active nature for service to others
- Learn to draw adventure into your life
- Grow accustomed to stability and fixed situations.

LIFE PATH : 6 – VISION & ACCEPTANCE

Your Life Path number identifies the challenges which you will face and the specific issues to be confronted on your journey through life. Remember that it will be necessary to overcome the negative expressions of your number energy to realise your highest potential.

The main theme in a life path #6 is the tendency to look for perfection in a far from ideal world instead of accepting and appreciating life exactly as it is.

Life Challenges:

As a 6 your tendency towards idealism and perfectionism will lead you into judgements about your own self-worth and ultimately to disappointment in others. Your high standards are not always grounded in reality and so the challenge for all 6's is to cultivate patience and perspective, and to see the perfection in life, here and now, as it unfolds. You should understand that you came here to work out the imperfections which are an inherent part of the human condition. Learn not to judge or be obsessed by small flaws and errors otherwise you will often be disheartened. 6's must be grounded in reality whilst striving to understand the bigger picture where everything is always as it should be. Be realistic and avoid petty obsession. Learn to go with the flow of life.

Positive Characteristics:

Loving / honest
Reliable / conscientious
Balanced / self sacrificing
Sympathetic / understanding
Sociable / generous

Negative Characteristics:

Smothering / unforgiving
Dependent / interfering
Inflexible / martyr
Craves appreciation / self righteous
Fussy / critical

The extent to which you embrace your life path will determine whether you are expressing and experiencing the negative or the positive aspects of your specific life energy.

Negative Expression: When life challenges are not faced or successfully resolved, your energy may be blocked, positive expression is repressed and the following problems may be experienced:

- Low self worth / tendency to judge
- Fear of appearing emotionally vulnerable
- Difficulty trusting others or relaxing and loosening up
- Difficulty in committing to relationships
- Suffocating outside pressure / asthma
- Outside pressure to conform
- Cold or detached persona
- Driven to seek perfection
- High expectations of others
- Confusion about inner feelings

Remedies:

- Learn that the only perfection is the flow of life as it is
- Tai Chi and Yoga will help to ground you
- Self assertiveness training
- Rise above the tendency to be conditional in your giving or smothering in your loving

LIFE PATH : 7 – TRUST & OPENNESS

Your Life Path number identifies the challenges which you will face and the specific issues to be confronted on your journey through life. Remember that it will be necessary to overcome the negative expressions of your number energy to realise your highest potential.

The main theme in a life path #7 is the need to trust in the spirit within, to open up and feel safe to share your inner beauty.

Life Challenges:

As a 7 you have a need for privacy with your own space and time to yourself because the inner process is more important to you than material achievement. However, you must learn to trust your own intuition and feelings even in the midst of difficulties. Only in this way will you be able to trust others and share your inner knowledge. 7's must find balance between solitude and companionship, rational mind and intuitive mind, external knowledge and inner wisdom. You must overcome your fear of betrayal by cultivating your capacity for intuitive discrimination. When doubts, anxiety and confusion arise, learn to communicate by clear expression.

Positive Characteristics:	*Negative Characteristics:*
Wise / philosophical	**Solitary / introverted**
Intelligent / deep thinker	**Secretive / gloomy**
Perceptive / refined	**Cynical / moody**
Observant / contemplative	**Suspicious / unsympathetic**
Eccentric / dry humoured	**Unhappy / sarcastic**

The extent to which you embrace your life path will determine whether you are expressing and experiencing the negative or the positive aspects of your specific life energy.

Negative Expression: When life challenges are not faced or successfully resolved, your energy may be blocked, positive expression is repressed and the following problems may be experienced:

- Obsessive need for privacy
- Idealised longing / rigid boundaries
- Emotional brittleness / tendency to withdraw
- Excessive fear of betrayal and broken trust

Remedies:
- Avoid too much solitude
- Cultivate companionship and the capacity for deep friendship with those who can stimulate and encourage your hidden potential.
- Look to express your inner wisdom in a practical way through creativity or artistic pursuits
- Extend your interests to include more of life culture and humanity
- Get out and enjoy your affinity with nature.

LIFE PATH : 8 – POWER & ABUNDANCE

Your Life Path number identifies the challenges which you will face and the specific issues to be confronted on your journey through life. Remember that it will be necessary to overcome the negative expressions of your number energy to realise your highest potential.

The main theme in a life path #8 is the need to reconcile your inner drive for material success and achievement with inner barriers against power and abundance.

Life Challenges:

Material success may come naturally to 8's, but only after you have resolved your inner conflicts concerning money, power, authority, control and recognition. Abundance is more an inner attitude than a sign of material success. As an 8 you may attract or repulse abundance according to your own sense of esteem and expression of inner energy. The challenge therefore will be to transcend negative feelings about yourself and your achievements, and then to seek to use success in positive ways for the highest good. Affluence and power are not incompatible with higher ideals, however, 8's must learn to balance extreme expressions of material success with generosity, wisdom and compassion.

Positive Characteristics:	Negative Characteristics:
Determined / assertive	Dominant / egotistical
Successful / visionary	Unscrupulous / demanding
Hardworking / business instincts	Manipulative / materialistic
Dependable / leader	Stubborn / seeks recognition
Tough / tenacious	Jealous / guilt ridden

The extent to which you embrace your life path will determine whether you are expressing and experiencing the negative or the positive aspects of your specific life energy.

Negative Expression: When life challenges are not faced or successfully resolved, your energy may be blocked, positive expression is repressed and the following problems may be experienced:

- Money difficulties
- Intimidation of others
- Money hunger / exaggerated poverty consciousness
- "Unlucky" accidents / illness
  - Lack of recognition
  - Aggression / power obsession
  - Low self worth / self sabotage
  - Family issues of pain and conflict

Remedies:
- Learn to see beyond the lure of the material world
- Learn to enjoy your gains, relax and have fun
- Learn how to channel your business acumen for higher expression
- Develop ethical practices based on fairness, benevolence and the aim of empowering others
- Broaden your interest in humanity and share your abundance with generosity

LIFE PATH : 9 – INTEGRITY & WISDOM

Your Life Path number identifies the challenges which you will face and the specific issues to be confronted on your journey through life. Remember that it will be necessary to overcome the negative expressions of your number energy to realise your highest potential.

The main theme in a life path #9 is the need to transcend rational mental thought and allow your intuitive wisdom to guide you and enable you to empower others.

Life Challenges:

As a 9 your main challenge is to align your life to integrity and intuition, to embrace spiritual principles and inspire others by your example. You have an inner longing to find your calling, but there are many obstacles which will cause frustration and guilt as you struggle with "cause and effect". 9's have charisma and an inner light which others will follow so you must understand the consequences of your own actions and learn to "walk the talk". You may be required to swim against the tide of convention and conformity, guided by your intuitive understanding of universal laws. You must cultivate the capacity for self-forgiveness as you continually try to release old patterns of self judgement and surrender to your highest notion of service to others.

Positive Characteristics:

Compassionate / tolerant
Mystical / intuitive
Magnetic / altruistic
Unconditional / inspirational
Healing / joyous

Negative Characteristics:

Idealistic / insensitive
Dreamy / vague
Melodramatic / over emotional
Gullible / victim complex
Over stretched / dissatisfied

The extent to which you embrace your life path will determine whether you are expressing and experiencing the negative or the positive aspects of your specific life energy.

Negative Expression:

When life challenges are not faced or successfully resolved, your energy may be blocked, positive expression is repressed and the following problems may be experienced:

- Frustration, guilt and harsh self criticism
- Chronic illness / back problems
- Rebellious tendencies / misguided idealism
- Rare afflictions or arthritis.

Remedies:

- Learn to forgive and accept yourself
- Overcome the sub-conscious need to punish yourself
- Cultivate structured thinking, concentration and practical application of ideas
- Become detached from the need for love or for personal satisfaction and reward
- Hypnosis can help to heal the sub-conscious

148

LIFE PATH : 11 – MASTER ILLUMINATION

Your Life Path number identifies the challenges which you will face and the specific issues to be confronted on your journey through life. Remember that it will be necessary to overcome the negative expressions of your number energy to realise your highest potential.

The main theme in a life path #11 is the need to express your highest vibration and raise the awareness of humanity through your insights and inspiration.

Life Challenges:

Master numbers impose the demand for self mastery. As an 11 your challenge is to work for the highest good and make your ideas practical and accessible to all. 11's must seek the lessons available to all humanity by facing the day to day challenges of relationships, jobs and money within the material world. You must learn to live honestly and with integrity as you teach the truth you have discovered. 11's must grow in self belief and overcome a deep insecurity, although you will be guided by a different, higher perception and spiritual focus.

Positive Characteristics:	*Negative Characteristics:*
Intuitive / sensitive	Over sensitive / insecure
Bright / creative	Nervous / impractical
Inspirational / visionary	Idealistic / fearful
Enthusiastic / humanitarian	Dissatisfied / dreamy

The extent to which you embrace your life path will determine whether you are expressing and experiencing the negative or the positive aspects of your specific life energy.

Negative Expression: When life challenges are not faced or successfully resolved, your energy may be blocked, positive expression is repressed and the following problems may be experienced:

- Blocked 11's will revert to the energy of number 2 in both the positive and negative aspects
- You may hand over power to others working with a narrower focus.

Remedies:
- Find inner peace by surrendering to higher ideals
- Cultivate meditation and contemplative practices to develop your inner resources
- Learn to express your creativity in practical ways which make higher knowledge accessible to all

LIFE PATH : 22 – MASTER BUILDER

Your Life Path number identifies the challenges which you will face and the specific issues to be confronted on your journey through life. Remember that it will be necessary to overcome the negative expressions of your number energy to realise your highest potential.

The main theme in a life path #22 is the need to express your highest vibration in order to build things for humanity through your organisation and planning.

Life Challenges:
Master numbers impose the demand for self mastery. As a 22 you have the challenges of a 2 – which are doubled through the expression of 22, as well as the challenges of a 4. The impact of a double 2 expression can bring challenges with sensitivity, intuition, harmony and relationships, whilst the 4 influence can bring challenges with hard work, discipline, practicality, building and organisation. A 22 has a desire to undertake big projects and set big goals. The lessons on this path are to harness the desire to build for the benefit of humanity as a whole, and to build something of lasting value for humanity.

Positive Characteristics:	*Negative Characteristics:*
Master builder	**Master Destroyer**
Organised	**Disorganised**
Hard working	**Lazy / Workaholic**
Disciplined	**Ill Disciplined**
Vision for Humanity	**Self Centred**

The extent to which you embrace your life path will determine whether you are expressing and experiencing the negative or the positive aspects of your specific life energy.

Negative Expression: When life challenges are not faced or successfully resolved, your energy may be blocked, positive expression is repressed and the following problems may be experienced:
- Blocked 22's will revert to the energy of number 4 in both the positive and negative aspects
- You can become a workaholic or over concerned with the detail and process
- Since 4 is the root number for health, when blocked, you could experience health issues

Remedies:
- Ensure that you are involved in building something of lasting value for humanity
- Ensure you have addressed the issues which underpin the 2 expression and the 4 expression
- Learn to express your creativity in practical ways which make higher knowledge accessible to all through whatever you build

150

LIFE PATH : 33 – MASTER HEALING LOVE

Your Life Path number identifies the challenges which you will face and the specific issues to be confronted on your journey through life. Remember that it will be necessary to overcome the negative expressions of your number energy to realise your highest potential.

The main theme in a life path #33 is the discovering of your healing energy by opening your heart and practicing unconditional love.

Life Challenges:

Master numbers impose the demand for self mastery. As a 33 your challenge is to willingly give yourself to others who need help, without being caught up in the pain of the world – remember, everything happens for a reason. The challenge for a 33 is to benefit and serve others. The influence of a double 3 makes a 33 extremely emotional. You must learn to master balance and detachment whilst practicing caring and giving to all who need it.

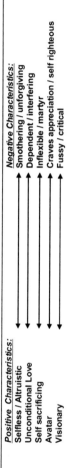

Positive Characteristics:	*Negative Characteristics:*
Selfless / Altruistic	**Smothering / unforgiving**
Unconditional Love	**Dependent / interfering**
Self sacrificing	**Inflexible / martyr**
Avatar	**Craves appreciation / self righteous**
Visionary	**Fussy / critical**

The extent to which you embrace your life path will determine whether you are expressing and experiencing the negative or the positive aspects of your specific life energy.

Negative Expression: When life challenges are not faced or successfully resolved, your energy may be blocked, positive expression is repressed and the following problems may be experienced:
- Blocked 33's will revert to the energy of number 6 in both the positive and negative aspects
- You take ownership of the problems of others, rather than help others take responsibility for their own issues / challenges

Remedies:
- Maintain focus on your overall vision for humanity
- Cultivate meditation and contemplative practices to develop your inner resources
- Learn to express your creativity in practical ways which make higher knowledge accessible to all
- Allow others to accept responsibility for their own issues / challenges

Acknowledgements

Many people have contributed to the writing of this book – either directly or indirectly. Over the years I have been inspired by ideas or concepts which have been proposed by other authors or speakers on this subject and whilst too numerous to mention, I would like to acknowledge the influence on this material and say thank you for having the courage to broadcast your ideas or to commit your ideas to paper.

All projects start with a spark of imagination, and this project is no exception. The critical point is whether that initial spark is stamped out or encouraged. I would like to thank Jack Black who not only recognised my vision for this project but also financed the early stages when this project was nothing more than embers, for this commitment I am truly thankful.

I would also like to thank Ray Holmes (the wise one) and Tom McFadyen who not only provided valuable input, but also acted as sounding boards throughout the project.

I would like to thank my son, Christopher, whose short life shaped much of the thinking in this book. And last, but by no means least, I would like to thank my wife Maureen and my daughter Emma for their continued love and support – especially through some dark times.

Printed in the United Kingdom by
Lightning Source UK Ltd., Milton Keynes
137435UK00001B/375/A